BEN

DIARY OF A HEROIN ADDICT –
A MOTHER'S FIGHT

M-Y BOOKS PAPERBACK

© Copyright 2016
Anne Rogers

A CIP catalogue record for this title is available from the British Library

ISBN–978-1-911124-25-2

Prologue

I sometimes delude myself into thinking that if I could have Ben back for just one day I'd get him clean. How stupid is that? He died six years ago at the age of 34, and for half of those years he was an addict. As for getting him clean, we spent 13 of those years trying to do just that.

Ben has gone. His death was one of no consequence and many would say 'good riddance to bad rubbish'. Even his inquest was attended only by the deputy coroner, his clerk, myself and my youngest daughter, Sarah. Our small village church had been packed for his funeral, however.

So why do I want to write his story? What was there about him that warrants the telling of it? Ben had been on drugs since the age of 17, half of his life. What had made him get into drugs in the first place and, above all, why couldn't he stop?

The remarkable thing about this story is the fact that Ben left behind a unique legacy of his drug addiction – almost 40 hours of film footage taken during the last four years of his life. In the few weeks leading up to his death, this was edited into a short documentary entitled "Sick and Tired of Feeling Sick and Tired", produced by Hanley Probation Services with the help of a young film maker, Darren Teale, from Junction 15 in Stoke-on-Trent. Two weeks after Ben died, Darren brought the film to show Ben's father and I, and affirmed Ben's wish to have it made public.

The film was incredibly harrowing and explicit, and our first reaction was to bury it and never let it be seen by anyone, let alone our family and friends. However, after a lot of thought and heart searching we agreed to release it to Darren to try to get it on television. Junction 15 sent it to Channel 4, who turned it down as they were in the process of making a documentary about the problem and couldn't take another on board.

That could have been it, but I wouldn't let it lie and became convinced that the film could be used to educate people. I thought that it could help the police see the other side of drugs, namely the victims of addiction, and the effect drugs have on the families of addicts. I also thought the film could greatly benefit the prison authorities and drugs agencies that, through no fault of their own, see only a part of the problem and rarely the full picture. From my personal experience, I also felt that the general public were largely ignorant to the many factors at play within drug addiction, choosing largely to focus upon the criminal aspect. I firmly believe that whatever the reason someone gets into drugs in the first place it very quickly becomes an illness. I also wanted families to be more open about having the problem within the family. Addiction needs to be outed by those it has affected most, and the secrecy and shame surrounding it can only exacerbate the problem. Finally, I felt that the film should be shown and discussed in schools, and that children should be taught that drugs are not an option, that at best drug use would destroy their looks and play havoc with their mental health and that at worst, as with Ben, it would kill them.

Ben was an addict. Drugs became his life and defined who he was. His life story should perhaps have ended with his funeral, but in a way it was only the beginning, and it is here that I must begin.

LIFE BEFORE DEATH

Chapter 1

Ben was born an addict. He was born sucking his thumb, and was an avid thumb sucker until one day at the age of seven he came home from school and announced he'd given it up, just like that. I laughed (was that 'bad' parenting?) and said 'wait until bedtime.' I was sure that once he was asleep the thumb would subconsciously go into his mouth, but he never put his thumb back in his mouth again, not even when he was sleeping. His strength of character emerged again in his early teens when he became a vegetarian, which was probably because we lived just up the road from a farm where his best friend's dad, a farmer, reared and slaughtered his own cows. He kept that up, even though the smell of bacon drove him up the wall, until his mid-twenties when he relapsed – a familiar phrase to addicts.

His dad and I had met whilst Mike was doing his national service stationed in my home city of Carlisle. We married in 1957 and, after a short spell living in Mike's hometown of Ludlow in Shropshire, we took the bold step of moving to London. We lived on the top floor of a very old block of flats in Railton Road, Brixton. Railton Road was in those days a hotbed of racial tension, with the police marshalling the rioting on horseback. I went back to revisit it recently and barely recognised the road. The block of flats had been demolished and although it was ten pm there were few people around and it all felt very calm and safe, not a bit like it was in the late 1960's. Our two eldest children, Stephanie and Sam, were born whilst we were living in Brixton, and I became interested in getting them into a local playgroup. No such facility existed at that time, so a friend and I set about trying to find premises. We eventually found an old disused school and contacted the Pre-School Playgroup Association, who made the dream a reality. As well as the playgroup facilities, there were also classes for mums to learn all kinds of parenting skills and I joined in as a volunteer playgroup leader. In 1964, Lambeth Council started up its first One O'clock Club in Brockwell Park in Brixton. This was a play facility designed to enable the under-fives to get out of their high-rise flats and enjoy outdoor activities in a safe environment. I was the first mother that they employed with pay, and when we eventually left London my job went to one of my very best friends, Peggy, who only recently retired from the post nearly 40 years later, so I know that the facility still thrives.

Mike worked in the exhibition industry at that time, but he wasn't happy living in London so he found a job in Fleetwood, Lancashire, and we moved there in 1965. It was in Blackpool that Sarah, my youngest daughter, and Ben were born, although Ben almost never was.

Ben was born in 1971 at a maternity hospital called Glenbrook in Blackpool. He was our fourth child but my fifth pregnancy. I had it all planned very early on in my married life. I would have four children: two close together, then a gap of five years and two more within 15 month periods. I am a very organised person, and my plans ran to perfection except I got knocked down by a car when I was three months into my fourth pregnancy, which resulted in me losing the baby. Not to be deterred, I became pregnant with Ben two years later. I can't begin to describe the joy that Ben's birth brought to us as a family, even though Sarah had just started school when I found out I was pregnant with Ben and Mike had recently left his secure job to become self-employed.

There were nine years between Ben and Sam, but Sam was delighted he had a brother and not another sister. The girls were ecstatic because in Ben they had a living, breathing doll to play with. No child was more wanted, and if you can spoil a child with love and attention then yes, Ben was spoiled. We all adored him and Mike and I had the perfect family – two girls and two boys. Mike and the doctor made sure there would be no more, however, and when I was still recovering from Ben's birth they conspired for Mike to have a vasectomy without consulting me. These were very early days for vasectomy operations. Mike had to pay for it, and he pleaded with me not to tell any of our friends. Imagine his horror when he was being prepped when he realised that the nurse in attendance was one of our neighbours! He had a bad reaction to the operation, resulting in a temporary limp which I had to tell friends was caused by him tripping up and falling down the stairs! Ben, whether I wanted it or not, was to be our last child.

Ben was a beautiful baby, as all babies are to their parents. He was 9lbs 1ozs at birth, nothing scrawny about him and, as I mentioned before, he was surrounded by five adoring fans. He spent the first three years of his life in Cleveleys, living just a stone's throw from the sea. Ben had the perfect early start: I didn't work and his siblings were all at school, which meant he had my undivided attention. His dad was now self-employed and had his studio in Cleveleys so Ben saw an awful lot more of his dad than his brother and sisters had at the same age, and he went to playgroup, as his siblings had before him.

Those were good days, really good days, especially the summer days spent building sandcastles on the beach and paddling in the sea. I was very aware of how fortunate my children were to be living where we were, and when I heard an appeal on the radio put out by the Children's Country Holiday Fund I leapt into action. The Children's Country Holiday Fund was a London-based charity that existed to arrange holidays in rural areas for children living in deprived situations in the inner city. I knew I could offer a brilliant holiday for such a child and started out by offering a holiday for a girl a little older than Steffi, who was seven at the time. When we went to meet Brenda she arrived off the train with two other children. The label pinned to her chest was parallel with my eyes – yes, she was very tall, 12 years old and cheeky with it. In fact she smoked like a trooper, and taught Steffi her first swear word! Brenda stayed with us for two weeks and I had a tough job getting her back on the train at the end of the holiday.

The experience got me going, though, and over the six weeks school summer breaks for the next three years I organised holidays for many children to travel from London to the Fylde Coast for two weeks at a time, always having one and sometimes two kids staying with us. I stopped doing it when Ben arrived, handing over the reins to my friend, Moire, who continued the good work for many years. They were very happy days for all of us.

Chapter 2

When Ben was nearly four years old, Mike was approached by Myotts, a pottery firm in Stoke-on-Trent that had been bought out by the American firm, Interpace. Mike must have met their design director through the big Gifts Trade Fair held every year at Earls Court in London but which spilled over into the Blackpool Winter Gardens. George, the American design director, wanted to return to the States and he was looking for someone to take over his position in the Potteries.

We talked it over in great depth. Steffi and Sam were teenagers, and therefore at tricky stages in their development. Steffi was settled into Fleetwood Grammar School and was adamant that she was not leaving. I almost agreed with her when Mike and I took a trip to Stoke-on-Trent so that we could see what our future habitat would be like. The steelworks were still up and running, and the potteries, of which there were many, were still flourishing, the result of which was a pall of smoke that hung heavy over the five towns. We parked our car outside what was then Lewis' department store and I actually cried at what I was seeing. We were considering leaving the seaside to come to this dark, depressing, Lowry landscape. Mind you I remember being equally depressed at the thought of moving to Blackpool from London. When I was 14 years old, I had gone to Blackpool on a bank holiday day trip with my mum, joining the throng on the Golden Mile. We decided to turn round and walk the other way but it was nigh on impossible, such was the crush of people. "I'm never going to Blackpool again as long as I live," I vowed to my mum and then ended up living six miles from it and loving it!

So what changed my mind? I would have to say that it was the Potteries people. I had moved around quite a bit in my married life, from Carlisle to Craven Arms, to Ludlow, to London and then to Cleveleys, but I had never encountered such open, friendly and cheerful people. The decision was made. Mike would accept the offer and move to Stoke ahead of us, and I would stay with the house until it was sold.

The company rented Mike a bungalow in Kidsgrove and he was there for the best part of a year while I tried to sell the house, which had been in a bad state of repair when we bought it and still needed lots doing to it at the point of sale. When we first moved to Cleveleys, it was into a semi-detached chalet bungalow, and we lived there for nine years before we moved to a large pre-war detached house just five minutes' walk from the sea front. It was going to be our dream home. "I am never going to move again," said I as I closed the door behind us on removal day. Famous last words, it turned out, as we were there for eighteen months only. We had done some work on the house and garden before Mike left for Stoke-on-Trent but the work was by no means completed, and of course when Mike came home at weekends there was little time, or energy, to build on that.

Mike missed his family and they of course missed him tremendously, so he started coming home midweek on Wednesday evenings, arriving late and leaving early the next morning. Weekends started to get fractious, and at one point Mike said he would pack the job in and come back home. For me though there was no turning back. Mike had secured a very good job that he enjoyed and we had to consider the future. If he left Myotts what was there to come back to in Cleveleys? Although he was never without work, it wasn't profitable and centred mainly around the entertainment business that was Blackpool.

Shortly after this upset, after I had put my foot down and insisted we carry on as we were, we found a buyer, at least until the survey showed that underneath the floorboards the property was afloat with water. Funnily enough, the survey we had to have done when we bought the property had not revealed anything of this nature. All was not lost though, because further investigation revealed that the water was tidal – it came and went! The sale went ahead and we were able to look for a property, but we had to do it quickly.

We looked at several houses in and around Burslem in Stoke-on-Trent where Myotts were situated, but nothing proved right, until a chap that Mike was working with told him about a cottage he knew of that was for sale in the village of Alton, some 14 miles from work. When we saw it we knew it was for us, although to be honest it was right at the top of our budget, £15,000. Our house in Cleveleys had sold for £13,750 and we never made a penny of profit on it. If you have seen Ben's DVD you will know why we fell in love with the cottage, it was picture perfect.

We moved to Alton in April 1975 with four children, two of whom were adamant they hated it and would move back to Cleveleys as soon as they were 16 years old – this was before Childline - and our two Siamese cats, Winston and Dougal, who were much less trouble.

If you asked me for my advice on what to do if your situation involved a teenager taking drugs, I wouldn't be able to advise you. I would say there is no right or wrong way to deal with it – I don't know whether it's better to keep the lines of communication open or to cast them adrift to sort themselves out. I would only say 'go with your gut reaction'. With regards to moving house with children, however, I would say 'never move a teenager from out of their environment, they won't take kindly to it'. Steffi and Sam's move into their new habitat is another story, however, and I'm here to tell you about Ben, who took to the move like a duck to water. That said, he was only three years old, and at three, home is where Mum and Dad are.

I very quickly got Ben into playschool and he loved it. He had some great playmates and these became his closest friends throughout primary school until he was nine years old. They played at each other's houses, joined Cubs together, celebrated birthdays, and all the other normal things that small children do when they interact. This continued until he reached nine, then suddenly all his friends moved up to middle school, leaving Ben behind because Ben's ninth birthday fell after the summer holiday school break. Ben never seemed to catch up with the 'big' boys.

My friend gave me a few photos of the group a little while ago that she had come across whilst clearing out some drawers and they did seem to verify what I have just written. Ben seems to be standing a little apart, or sitting withdrawn from the rest of the group. Looking at them was painful for me, not just because of Ben's perceived isolation but also because all the boys have successful, happy lives – why not Ben? Or should it be 'why Ben'? I know that some of the boys also dabbled in drugs when they were young, but it didn't become the consuming problem that it became for Ben. Ben used to say he had an addictive personality and that possibly was a factor, but if a personality is not typically 'addictive' then the person can nonetheless become an addict. He was always in trouble at primary school, either that or the headmaster fancied me, because the head was nearly always waiting for me when I went to pick Ben up after school. It was always trivial little boy naughtiness, but the most serious incident was that he and another seven year old had been caught trying to light a cigarette in the boy's toilet. "He could have burnt the school down," was the headmaster's lament. Ben got a smack when I got him home – you could smack your child in those days.

Ben's account:*My father came home first and, although I shouldn't say this as mum would not want to hear, it was my father I'd tell the problem to first every time. Dad listened before blowing his top, if he blew his top at all. One thing for certain with dad there would always be a forgiveness and an "I love you Benj". As I started to tell dad the phone started ringing and in walked mum. It didn't take long for my teacher to break the news to mum and then the fireworks began! My mum made me smoke one of my dad's cigarettes in front of her and, of course, I had to do the pretend coughing and say how nasty and smelly it tasted. They weren't to know I was already smoking and liking it. My dad, however, wouldn't accept my apology that night which was a measure of the amount of trouble I was in. He just said "you've really let me down today Ben". He took it on himself that it was his fault – I smoked because he did. It wasn't. I was grounded for weeks, grovelling to try and get liberated. I was essentially a 'good boy', if I was told I had to stay in then I wouldn't escape and cause ructions and mountains of worry. I had a lot of love and respect and still do for my parents during childhood and teens, even if my own self worth, which is low, stopped me showing my feelings for them in return. As a family we've never been ashamed to show and speak 'love' to one another and I thank them for that. At least I'll always know love.*

Other occasions at primary school are faint in my memory. I remember always being pretty much the class live wire, all through schooling in fact. I certainly had a smart answer for everything which on many occasions made me unpopular with the authoritarian figures. Only as I got older and more mellow did I learn more about how people should be played or what was expected of me. I had a good education and because of my personality was never short of friends. People want to be around people that 'buzz' but once that buzz goes they move on.

Chapter 3

Ben's reputation seemed to follow him from primary to middle school to senior school. It was as if they had him sussed before ever he set foot in the school. I remember him crying once when he was in high school because he was convinced he had improved that year but we had returned from the school open evening with a bad result. "It doesn't matter what I do, it's never good enough," he cried. Steffi, who has spent all her working life with children with learning difficulties, believes that if Ben was going through the school system now he would probably have been diagnosed with ADHD, but when Ben was young he was just labelled disruptive and naughty.

Sarah's recollections:

My early memories of Ben are patchy as I was not yet five years old when he was born. I had been the youngest and was very happy in that role but I remember feeling only great joy that we had a new member in our family and very proud of my little brother. My parents always seemed to have enough time and energy for all four of us individually and it is a huge testimony to them that growing up as an adult I never felt jealous of Ben or angry that he was taking so much from them.

My last memory of Ben is total sadness. I went to the detox unit on the afternoon of his death to be with Mum and Dad, and we were allowed to spend some time with him. I think we were all in shock, not because his addictions had finally killed him but because he was in a hospital bed and we couldn't comprehend how, less than 24 hours after his admittance, he was dead. I remember Mum and I commenting on how beautiful he looked; somehow his good looks had returned, he looked very peaceful and he was smiling.

My life as Ben's sister is divided very firmly into three parts. Our early life was very much like that of any other family. He was very lively, so full of life and lots of fun. He was possibly more of a handful than the rest of us – there was a big age gap between him and Steffi and it was sometimes as if he was trying to be older than he was. Like all of us though, he was loved for who he was and I'm so grateful for that time.

As a teenager, he became very aware of his good looks and charm. I used to gel and blow-dry his hair for him before school, spending more time on his appearance than on my own! It was at this time that Ben had a few incidents where he got drunk, which horrified Mum and Dad as he was so young. I just thought it was another example of Ben trying to act older than he was and didn't worry too much.

The second part was learning to live with the problem. I don't remember Mum and Dad ever telling me that Ben was on drugs but I remember vividly the day that I knew. Ben had gone to college in Leicester and at that time I was working in a travel agency. He came into the shop one afternoon and stood shaking in the corner. It took minutes for me to realise that it was him, he looked gaunt and ill and he'd dyed his hair blond – I just did not recognise him. From that afternoon until the day that he died I was never to have peace of mind about Ben again.

When I got married I spent weeks beforehand stressing about how my Mum would be when I moved out as we are so close. As it happened, the morning after our wedding we had a knock on the door only to find a distraught Mum and Dad who'd just come from the hospital. Ben had tried to kill himself.

There was the time when I was 39 weeks pregnant and Ben phoned me at 1.00am to tell me that he'd failed with his 'cold turkey' once again and that he couldn't carry on any more. I stayed on the phone with him until 5.00am, begging him to stay talking with me so that I knew he was still with us. Incidents like these caused horrendous rows with my husband.

Through all of the very bad times though there are many good memories. Ben was very loving and when he was well he was funny and charismatic. He was a fantastic uncle to my two children and tried so hard all through his addict life to still be a part of our family.

My last afternoon with Ben sums up how much he loved us I think. It was Dad's birthday, and Dad was terminally ill and in a lot of discomfort. Phil and I decided to buy him a hammock so that he could rest in the garden but it had to be built. It was a boiling hot day and Ben must have been so uncomfortable – he had deep vein thrombosis, circulatory problems, a really sore ulcerated mouth and the most horrible skin rash, but he was so enthusiastic and was determined to help Phil set it up for Dad. It is such a bittersweet memory for me now, seeing Ben's huge swollen fingers trying to tighten screws and bolts so that Dad could rest. He was in such good humour too; it was a lovely, precious afternoon.

It was on that day that Mum told me that Ben had booked himself into rehab in two weeks' time. I remember just feeling relieved that Mum would have some respite from Ben and a lot of quality time with Dad. I don't think it even registered that Ben might now get better, but I didn't believe he would die either.

The third part of my life has been living without Ben. I think I always tried to prepare myself that Ben could die from his addictions, and in some ways life is much easier now that he has gone. I understand better now that Ben was ill, it was no longer a choice for him, and I wish that I could have had that knowledge when he was still with us. He has taught me more than anyone else not to ever judge people and to see things differently, and I hope it's made me a better person. I miss him every day but it helps me to remember that he died smiling and I believe that he was happy to leave it all behind him.

Ben's childhood was a very normal one and I believe a happy time for all of us in the days before Ben got into real trouble. In middle school he was in the school orchestra playing a tuba which was almost as big as he was. He also taught himself to play guitar and was very keen on the music of the day. He was very into clothes and appearance even before he went to senior school, and I remember him asking if he could have his hair shaved off just prior to a concert he was playing in for the school at the JCB theatre. We, of course, said "no, definitely not," but as we were walking to the theatre from the car I noticed that Ben was walking backwards. I grabbed him, spinning him round only to find he'd shaved the hair off on the back of his head – he was always a chancer and he probably earned himself another smack then.

At high school he played cricket and football and, in fact, played in the village football team, a football team that prided itself on never winning a match! The team consisted mainly of a group of men some years older than Ben, probably well into their twenties to Ben's 16. There was a lot of socialising involved at one of the men's homes. This man was a professional photographer and Mike knew him quite well, so we had no need to be too concerned and there were other teenagers in the team too. I do believe on reflection that this was the start of Ben's real problems.

When Ben was 16 he went missing. He was gone for two weeks and we didn't know where. Mike went round to the photographer's home only to be told that Ben had gone off with one of the older men who had recently separated from his wife and children. This man was a drinker, and although we were assured that they would be fine and that it was just a camping trip, we were furious with the man and frantic with worry. This was before mobile phones and we had no contact whatsoever, no way of knowing if Ben was safe. We had two weeks of terrible concern, but sure enough Ben arrived back home, though in a sad and sorry state. He wouldn't explain where he'd been or what he'd been up to but I suspect it was a drinking spree.

The older man that Ben had gone off with ended up hanging himself just a few months later, and the photographer was killed in a dreadful road accident in the States just one year later whilst Ben was still with us. A third man, with whom, Ben shared accommodation for a short time, died from alcoholism in 2006. Ben went to this man's funeral only two weeks before he himself died. He was not well by this time, but was determined to go and pay his respects, and I have to say he made a real effort with his appearance, borrowing one of his Dad's jackets.

Chapter 4

Ben was obviously anxious to leave home and I suspect it was because he wanted to do things he knew we wouldn't put up with. I learned later that he had a drink problem that had started when he was just twelve years old. We had been invited to a friend's silver wedding party and, of course, Ben was included in the invitation. One of his school friends was in charge of an extremely large bowl of punch, which looked harmless with all the fruit floating on the top but was, as it turned out, loaded with spirits. Ben, aided and abetted by his friend, drank until he couldn't stand up and we were alerted to the problem by another guest that Ben was outside hanging over the drain with his fingers down his throat being sick. We took him home and he was out of it for almost 24 hours.

You would have thought he'd learnt his lesson from this, but no, I suspect Ben had a problem with drink from an early age although he was very good at keeping it from us. Once or twice we were called out to collect him from a party but at home in those school years he kept it well hidden from us. We did have quite a bit of alcohol in the house but I didn't drink at all and Mike only very occasionally. However, I did notice that drink was disappearing and I questioned Mike about it. He was adamant he hadn't drunk it but treated it like a joke. I was reduced to marking the bottles but still it was going down. I thought maybe Mike was enjoying a drop in his and his friend, our neighbour's, cups of tea, or maybe even Phil, Sarah's then boyfriend but now husband, was sneaking it.

I never thought it could be Ben, not once. Later when we learned the truth it caused quite a rift between Mike and I because I thought he'd treated it lightly, as a joke. He knew it wasn't him so he should have made it his business to find out who it was. I still get upset now when I think of it.

Ben's account:

I got involved in alcohol at a very early age. I'd steal whisky, gin (which I hate) vodka and any other spirit available. Often being found drunk and picked up by friends of my parents or, the worse scenario, by my folks themselves.

I had a bad experience put upon me by a so called family friend at a very early age. Although this is no excuse, and neither do I use it now, it affected me. At 12 I was smoking dope. I spent too much time hanging around adults. With everything that has happened in my life I was treated as an equal by these people. I was an adult in a child's body. I was taking magic mushrooms, acid, base, speed, barbits and within a few years was injecting diazepam eggs. The only things that stopped me buying these 50p knockouts was the fact I saw a programme about junkies in Glasgow losing limbs.

Sex was a big part of my early years – I lost my virginity at 13 and was not only in different drunken relationships each weekend , but was involved in sex with not only my own age group but with my older friends. I felt and still do feel a lot of guilt for the friends, alive and dead, that I hurt. Some things you can never forget or forgive. I can't.

Ben was a handsome youth and very popular with the girls. I think he probably had more girl friends than male friends, and in his life he had three serious relationships, all girls he had gone to school with. They all featured prominently in his adult years but I suspect they had all fallen in love with the young teenager from school.

Ben had developed a friendship in our village with a boy who was a year older than he was and who also went to Alleynes High School with him. Alex was a Goth and Ben hero-worshipped him. Alex dyed his hair black, wore lots of black leather and chains and, more importantly, could play a guitar and write music. Alex and Ben started making music together, and the day came when Ben walked in and said, "Alex and I are moving to London to make it in the music industry." Ben, incidentally, was still just 16, and there was no way his dad and I were going to allow him to cut loose like that. There was a big argument, lots of big arguments, and we even roped in Alex's mum to try to talk some sense into him – that he was too young, that he could perhaps go when he was older. I don't think Ben ever really forgave us for robbing him of the opportunity of becoming a rock God. Alex went without him and had some success. He formed a group called 'Fudge Tunnel' (don't ask) and they had an underground following of sorts. I remember going to Nottingham at some point and coming back with a 'Fudge Tunnel' tee shirt for Ben.

Alex is now a successful music producer in America and I have to say, hand on heart, Ben never resented Alex's success, but I know he thought he might have been up there with him. Maybe in retrospect it might have been better if we had let him go then, but we weren't to know that what lay ahead far exceeded the fears we had for him at that time moving to London.

Ben's comment:

Magic mushrooms had become a local discovery to me. Alton Towers had two massive fields on the draw up to its entrance. I discovered them there whilst walking through them with my mate, D. I said 'ever tried strong drugs?' He said 'not yet'. I pointed down to our feet surrounded by the bloody things. We filled our pockets and got home as quick as possible. The next five hours changed our lives – purple puddles everywhere, electric teeth, growing wallpaper, fuck – what a breakthrough. From there on we grazed often on our hands and knees in the fields. One night when I got home late my parents were waiting, "what's going on Ben, look at you", "nothing" I replied through chattering clenched teeth, mushrooms hanging from each side pocket and a large bag in one hand. I just needed to rest but, of course, everyone knows rest is impossible on a psychedelic high!

Chapter 5

As I have already said, Ben was desperate to leave home but his GCSE results were poor and he didn't want to go into the sixth form, so he got a placement in Birmingham that only lasted twenty four hours before he landed back home again. Within a week or so he managed to get on a printing course at a college in Leicester. Because of my job working in social housing, I was able to help get him a Housing Association bedsit which was barely bigger than my kitchen table!

Ben completed the one year course and got a job as a silk screen printer with a printing company in Leicester. This was in the days before mobile phones and computer networking sites, so communication was sparse. Occasionally he'd phone and we'd write to him. Mike probably paid him a couple of visits en-route to somewhere with his work but we had no reason to think it wasn't working out for him. Then one day, I had a phone call at work from his company to say they hadn't seen Ben for a week – did we know what was happening? I was trying to get hold of Mike when Ben walked through the door, soaking wet and thinner than I had ever known him, his hair dyed blond. He was shaking and visibly upset. "Don't make me go back Mum, I can't go back, please don't make me."

What was his problem? Ben only ever told us what he wanted to tell us and I know he didn't always tell us the truth, so we just had to accept what he said, which was, "I'm lonely, I have no friends, my bedsit has been broken into and my things were stolen, I'm scared there," and so on. I think they may have been thieves with taste, however, because they didn't take his record collection. I think the truth of the matter was that he was drinking heavily and possibly had started smoking cannabis, if he hadn't started already, and that unclassified drugs were maybe now in the frame.

Ben's account:

I was accepted onto a printing course in Birmingham and I moved into a house in Aston. Although I was only there one night I'll never forget it. The street had several burnt out cars parked up. The downstairs windows to the house were boarded up. There was no electricity and to top it all, the woman in the flat next door said in her Brummy accent, "I hope you're insured love, plenty of break-ins here", and sure enough that night the local burgling element wanted the squat and everything that was inside it, i.e. my belongings. I shouted for help but, of course, no-one arrived. I had tongues sticking through the holes in the window boards. It scared the living daylights out of me. It would have been less traumatic if they had burst in and whacked me but they were taunting me instead. I pleaded that I was a poor student with nothing but a few records and an Afghan coat. It turned out to be one of the longest nights of my life and so began my misfortunes with anything associated with Birmingham.

The next day the college course collapsed, which is just as well because I couldn't have stayed in the bedsit. My dad picked me up and in a whirlwind week I was enrolled at Southfield's School of Printing in Leicester and living in a housing association block. Several other prison looking cells all containing one or two people, a shared kitchen and bathroom – it was horrible, ground floor too. It had a bed and a chair, nothing more. I soon cluttered it and for the next year took absolutely no pride in it whatsoever. I hated it. I quickly got my grant and ploughed through it. I think they gave me £1000 a term which was impossible to survive on so I decided to spend it and die instead. I rolled into college lectures maybe two or three days a week and made some excuse up as to where I'd been for the rest of the week. I was very surprised to say the least when I passed my exams at the end of the year.

Obviously we couldn't make Ben go back to his job in Leicester and, with the state he was in, we really didn't want to send him back and so he came home, the first of many times he'd retreat into the safety of his family. He was not yet 18.

He was with us then for the next three years and it was a chaotic time, with three different jobs, two run-ins with the police, a suicide attempt, a six-month spell living with his newly married brother, Sam, and his wife, Jayne, in Newcastle-upon-Tyne, and the start of his first real relationship. All three jobs were with printing firms, the first two lasting no more than twelve months and the last even less, just a few weeks. I remember he went off to work as usual to this last position which was situated on the other side of the potteries, possibly a 16 mile journey, when the phone rang. Ben had got so far and then had just frozen. He couldn't drive any further because he was having a panic attack. Mike had to go out and get him. That was the end of that job.

This I think was the first sign of the mental state he was getting into. From then on until he died he suffered from anxiety, depression, paranoia, panic attacks and sleep deprivation – all a result, I believe, of his drugs habit.

Mike and I were at our wits end with him and I came home one day to find him taping up his car in the garage in order to gas himself. He cried, oh how he cried – enough tears for us to paddle in. We called in our doctor, who immediately got him a bed in St Edward's, the nearest hospital that dealt with mental breakdowns. Ben went in offering no resistance, but he didn't get much further than assessment because he walked out a few days later saying "they're all mad in there." This coming from someone who had scratched a cross into his forehead!

We had two weddings in the family in 1990. Sarah and Phil were married in Alton in July and Sam and Jayne in Lancaster in August. Joyous family occasions, or they would have been if Ben hadn't been such a worry. Sarah's wedding day was glorious weather-wise. The sun shone and family and friends gathered to celebrate in our church, which is just around the corner from where we live. We have walked that short walk several times over the years. We followed Steffi's baby son, Joseph's, tiny white coffin. Joe had died of a cot death and Ben was to have been his godfather. We have had six grandchildren baptised there over the years, and then in 2006 Ben's funeral, followed nine weeks later by Mike's. Joy and sorrow but even when the occasion was joyous Ben managed to spoil it.

He was at the wedding with his good friend, Max. Max and Ben had been friends for several years, and they remained friends for many more. What I didn't know was that they were both by this time involved in taking drugs. Max came to see me a year after Ben died and said he was going into rehab to get clean once and for all, that he wanted to live to see his son grown. Sadly, I went to his funeral in 2011 and the coroner reported that Max, a former heroin user, had turned to prescription drugs to help him beat his addiction and that a combination of drugs taken throughout his life had contributed to his death. Max was interviewed when Sky made the documentary on Ben and it's very telling that Max says "families, what do families know?"Ben got a bit stupid at the wedding through drinking too much but the real trouble came later. Mike and Ben had gone to bed but I had stayed up to unpick the hems of the borrowed underskirts that Sarah and my little granddaughter, Abby, were wearing. I was probably on a bit of a natural high after a lovely day, and I felt happy that my youngest daughter was now married to the man she loved and had loved since she was 17 years old. It was about 1.00 am and I had nearly finished when Ben came downstairs, walked into the lounge and sat down beside me. His mood was dark, he was very restless and he kept getting up and down. I made him a cup of tea and said he should get back into bed again. As he walked through the door he turned and said, "You will come and say goodnight to me, won't you mum?" I said I would and off he went. I could so easily have ignored that request as it was some time later before I went upstairs but true to my promise I went in to say goodnight.

Ben had been prescribed antidepressants and he'd taken the lot. I didn't know how many were in the bottle but the bottle was empty. I tried to rouse him but he was floppy and unresponsive. I ran to wake Mike and together we had to drag him to his feet, down the stairs and into the car in order to rush him to the hospital in Stoke-on-Trent. He was a dead weight, literally. The A & E was quiet as it was about 3.00 in the morning but Ben was creating a lot of fuss and we were called into the cubicle to try and persuade him to let the nurse put the tube down his throat to wash out his stomach. We asked the doctor if he was going to be alright but the doctor wasn't very sympathetic towards us, and said, "he may or may not recover, we'll have to wait and see.," Not what we needed to hear. They kept Ben in for 24 hours' observation and for an assessment of his mental health. Mike and I ended up knocking on Sarah and Phil's door – it was the first day of their new life together.

I remember also our other trip to A & E, to the same hospital, part of the hospital complex in which Ben died. It was a New Year's Eve, and Ben was only just out of his teens. We had a phone call prior to the midnight hour from a friend that Ben had been out with. They had stayed in the village to see the New Year in and gone to The Wild Duck, a very respectable hotel and bar very close to home. Apparently Ben had upset someone whilst drinking and when he and his friend left several lads jumped on Ben and stamped on his face. His friend, instead of bringing him home, took him straight to the hospital in Stoke and then phoned us.

When Mike and I got to the A & E department it was a bit like a battlefield, with young men and girls all over the corridor bleeding, crying and drunk. I remember thinking 'how do the staff cope with this lot, some of them incapable of standing up?' I could hear screams coming from one of the cubicles, which kind of distracted us from what was going on all around us. I never thought it was Ben, but it was. What a mess his face was in, it looked as though he had gone ten rounds with Mike Tyson, but the worst sight was his top lip. The nurse had stitched it up very carelessly, without anaesthetic, and I think I could have made a better job of it myself. Who can blame her though, it was New Year's Eve, all the patients there had injuries caused through excessive drinking and the staff were being verbally abused right, left and centre. He received no treatment for his eyes, which were so swollen he could barely open them, for his broken nose, or for the swelling to his face that was so bad I could hardly recognise him when he stumbled back into the hospital corridor.

Ben threatened to overdose twice after that and the last time in desperation I got a glass of water, poured the tablets onto the palm of my hand and said to him, "Come on then, I'll help you, go on Ben, take them." He didn't, as the threats were just a cry for help, but we were powerless to help him.

Chapter 6

Sam and Jayne, who had recently married and were living in Newcastle, where Sam was doing an M.A. and paying his way by working at the Newcastle General Hospital mopping out operating theatres, valiantly offered us a life line. Sam said, "Let Ben come and stay with us, he needs to get away from Alton into a new environment, it will be good for him and you need the break." We were so grateful to them, there they were just starting off their life together but were prepared to have a disturbed 20 year old move in for an indeterminate period, which turned out to be six months.

I know that in those six months Sam and Jayne did their very best to straighten Ben out. There was a lot of social mixing with their friends and many trips to the great outdoors. Sam and Jayne are great fell walkers and, living so close to the Lake District, they probably dragged Ben along with them, but to give Ben his due he went along with it and, I am sure, came to enjoy the experience. I know this because he really got into books to do with mountains, especially those in the Himalayas, mountaineering and climbers, dead or alive. His wishes for the scattering of his remains after his death were all to do with what he learned in his time with Sam and I am so pleased that we were able to carry those wishes out.

I think the breaking point came when Sam was returning home one night having done a late night shift at the hospital to see a crowd gathered in the road ahead. It was obvious that someone was flat on the ground because there was a pair of feet sticking out between the legs of the onlookers. Sam looked at these feet and thought, "those look just like Ben's trainers," and Ben's trainers they were! Ben was stretched out, head bleeding, blind drunk. Enough was enough and Ben returned home yet again.

Ben entered into his first serious relationship soon after he came back from Newcastle with a girl he had known since his middle school days. Marie lived in Uttoxeter with her parents and, like Ben, had no job. Mike and I liked her, and she seemed very quiet although her appearance gave the opposite impression. Marie had a fair amount of 'face furniture', and a rather attractive tattooed amulet around her upper arm. Mild by today's standards, but it drew attention in the early nineties. They didn't live together locally but they made the decision that they wanted to move to the Lake District, an area Ben had fallen in love with whilst staying with Sam and Jayne, who were themselves living near to Kendal. Off they went in Ben's battered old 2CV and got themselves a bedsit in Lancaster. They also acquired a kitten at that time, a tortoiseshell that they named Cale after the musician JJ Cale. Cale lives with me still, all I have left of Ben really. She's over 20 now and, like me, showing signs of wear and tear.

Amazingly, they then got a job. They had seen it advertised in the local paper, applied, got an interview and landed it. I couldn't believe it, they looked so outlandish, Marie with her 'face furniture' and Ben with his hair in dreadlocks! They were taken on by the Duchy of Lancaster's estate at Forton, near Lancaster; Ben as groundskeeper and gardener which, believe it or not, he loved doing and was quite good at, and Marie to change the beds and clean the fishing lodges on the estate. Best of all, there was a house to go with the job. We were all thrilled for them and felt this was the opportunity that could turn Ben round. We went to visit several times and he took great pride in showing us around the gardens. Marie was a real little home maker too, decorating and stencilling the walls. They even acquired a Border collie pup. Mike and I were able to sleep easy for a while.

The job lasted about 18 months but then Ben and Marie had a big fall-out and Marie returned to her parents in Uttoxeter. Ben was trying to do both the gardening and the fishing lodges but was definitely unstable in himself. I remember one night him ringing me, it was very late. Mike was away from home with work and I was ill with some stomach upset. Ben was on the other end of the phone crying and pleading with me to come but I just couldn't do the drive. As soon as Mike returned we went up to Forton to see for ourselves what was going on. When we got there he didn't answer the door although we knocked and knocked. We walked round to the window and saw him totally out of it on the settee. We got in through forcing a window and were horrified to find what we were later told to be cannabis plants strewn everywhere. Ben had had an old school friend come to visit a few days before and he had been so angry with the state that Ben was in and the fact that Ben had been cultivating the plants upstairs that he'd furiously smashed them up. Needless to say Ben was very quickly back home with us again.

Ben and Marie were reconciled and they took on the tenancy of a little cottage in Oakamoor, just two miles from Alton. The next thing that they hit us with was that Marie was pregnant. It was planned they said, it was what they wanted. Ben was absolutely over the moon. "This is what I need Mum, this will sort me out." We pledged our support to the both of them and I dared to believe that perhaps a baby would be good for Ben and would give him responsibility for someone other than himself. Then Marie decided to terminate her pregnancy. Ben was distraught, even following her to the clinic where Marie had the abortion begging her to change her mind. Looking back now, I am so glad Ben never had a child. What sort of life would that child have had now? I very much doubt that a baby would have been the answer to Ben's problems.

This caused serious problems in their relationship and, once again, Sam and Jayne came to the rescue. They had for many months been planning a trip to India. It would be a year away from home and they would travel extensively, meeting up at various locations with friends who were already there, or would be when Sam and Jayne were backpacking. Their plans went very wrong, however, because they had no sooner landed in Delhi when Jayne's dad had a serious stroke and they had to fly back. It was three months before they were able to return but whilst they were back in England they suggested that Ben fly out and join them for a month. Sam has written elsewhere in this book a little about Ben in India, but the following is some of Ben's writing:

> *After leaving Marie and my parents at the airport I entered into what must have been one of the longest, shittiest journeys of my life - 'mission Aeroflot' ....*
>
> *Delhi airport was a cool place. I changed £50 and had this great handful of notes in return, and then there was Sam and Jayne. To be fair, Sam and Jayne had saved for this trip for years and here was I, someone they had had little to do with except for a six month period a*

couple of years before in which I wreaked havoc into their sensible lives. They had grown up and were on a soul searching trip, whereas I on the other hand had recently recovered from a breakdown and a short stay at the local institution for the mentally unstable, heading there for time away from Marie to make a few decisions on the back of the sale of my 2CV. They had invited me to join them, this was a great risk to their dream.

I took a taxi and a rickshaw ride to where they were staying in Paraganj at the "Anoop" where funnily enough Nick was staying too – it was his regular stay. I deposited my bags in the room that we were all three sharing!

Ben had met Nick on the plane going out and they had connected.

I headed for the streets. Nick was also heading out and I joined him. Before I could take in all the wonderful colours and scents, Nick headed up a narrow alley opposite the hotel. We entered a small shop where Nick was greeted with open arms. We were told to take our shoes off and sat down with an Italian girl who was slipping in and out of sleep, and Haj, a Kashmiri, who promptly closed the door behind us. This was no ordinary shop. "What you needing Mr Nick" said Haj. Nick promptly told him a gram of brown and a toller of hash. "None of your tourist rubbish mind you or I won't be back". He talked to him with such rudeness I thought we'd be shown the door. "Mr Nick would I give the shits to you". Nick looked over to me and we burst into laughter. It broke the tension, after all I was on the other side of the world in an opium den with three strangers.

He disappeared into the back and returned with a wrap of paper and a great big 10 gram lump of hash. "Mr Nick, only the best for you". 1000 rupees if you please". Nick pulled a wad of money out of his pocket, "here's 950, take it or leave it". He took it and we were already off down the main bazaar looking for a shop that sold foil. Nick kept telling me that he only did it as a treat each time he returned to Delhi. I didn't care. I'd done that many other drugs in my life I figured this one would just be one more experiment. I was nervous though and the heat was intense. I'd never before sweated that way, drip, drip, it was the only time I remember that my eyelids were sweating.

Ten minutes or so later we were back in Nick's room, number 211 if I remember correctly. Marble was the décor, walls, floor, bathroom and no windows. All there was in the way of air conditioning was one of those great big fans in the centre of the ceiling which we couldn't turn on because of the gold dust we were about to take.

Nick rolled a piece of foil round a pen and said "there's the tooter" and proceeded to put a very small amount of gear onto the foil. I said "sure, that's enough", Nick just looked up and smiled. Holding a lighter under the foil I was fascinated to see this powder change form into a thick black resin that ran from one side of the foil to another as he moved the lighter. At last it was my turn, my first encounter with Lady Heroin. Of course if I'd know then what I know now I'd have run out of that room as quickly as I'd run into it.

I loved it, a thick cloud came over my head. I was encased in cotton wool. I had one line, two, then three and lay back. As the feeling washed over my bitter and angry soul, all the pain, all the confusion and all the misery I had felt and inflicted on my loved ones washed and drifted away. Slipping in and out of semi consciousness, all the worries I was feeling – Marie, suicide, slashed wrists, overdoses, money, fear – none of it mattered. Just for that moment I experienced real love. I'd found something that understood, that didn't want all I could give without it ever being enough. Then all of a sudden extreme nausea. I raced to the toilet and threw up like never before. I rose to the sink and washed my face repeatedly with cold water and looked into my soul in the mirror. Even the vomit was the nicest vomit I'd ever tasted.

Of all the stages in my life I can honestly say I was never really in control. I'd find something that appealed to me, that I enjoyed, and I'd abuse it until it became a problem and usually it was something that would take little effort – like drugs and love. I'm not saying there wasn't anything else in my life – that I didn't have a personality, or that I didn't care about the loved ones in my life for example, but maybe I was too sensitive, maybe I had too many fears and maybe, just maybe, I was too scared to grow up. At this stage in my life I didn't know what it was about my childhood that went wrong, it was only later when I'd visited a hypnotherapist that that would come to light, but I knew I was different, something had happened, something had gone wrong. I was always going to be that little boy looking up at the nasty people that would always fill me with fear, with guilt, with something other than what I should be. I was different, of course. I'd come from a wonderful family that were decent people who had worked hard all their lives to give, not just me, but all four of us the best start *in life and here I was, already with years of self abuse behind me blaming everyone but myself for my problems. It was her, she did it to me, it was him being unfair, but it wasn't... it was me, a time bomb waiting to go off. India was a chance to humble myself ....*

Chapter 7

Ben and Marie's relationship didn't survive long after India, with Marie moving out of the cottage whilst Ben was at work one day and leaving him to discover that she had gone when he got back that night. Ben moved back in with us and continued working in pottery retail. India had introduced him to 'chasing the dragon', but this didn't satisfy him for long, and the next step was injecting ...

Ben writes:*I'd only been back from India several weeks. I'd picked up with Marie again, forgiving but not forgetting the termination which had prompted the trip. I was drinking hard, bottles of spirits to sleep, pills and drink again to rise – life had returned to its stressful same. England had got to me again. My anxiety attacks were constant after years of pills, acid, mushrooms and speed, my body was not adjusting.*

I longed to be back in India – sun, monsoons, manic lifestyles and, of course, heroin. I never got hooked there, it just took the pain away.

I was socialising with a guy called 'Weasel' as he was known. He was about 27 years old and was from a public school boy background. He knew about my drug habits and once or twice we did coke. Late one night we decided to get hold of some brown. I was mind blown by this guy – money, rich friends and many contacts. It proved to me that you could have it all.

We hopped into his landrover and headed to a suburb of Stoke-on-Trent. We drove up a small lane until we got to a wooden bungalow at the end. We went up to the front door and the dogs went wild. Two overgrown rottweilers/pit bull terriers crossed and a bitch alsation which had to be chained always.

The noise brought a rush of three men racing round the corner covered in shit. 'Animal, Animal, it's me' shouted Weasel. "Oh fucking hell youth, thought you were raiding. Come round the back". The back of the bungalow had about 30 dogs kennels. Apparently his Nan used to board dogs there. Behind these kennels were fields, completely flooded out, they looked like paddy fields. It was dark with a beam shining from the roof of another landrover in the centre of the field directly in front of us. It had sunk and they were trying to free it with planks of wood under the wheels, but they were sinking too of course, hence the shit!

We went in through the back door. Animal and Weasel exchanged awkward politeness. Animal had awful asthma after smoking for 15 years. He looked like Animal from the Muppets, hence the name, and he was one of the first smack heads in the area.

We bought £30's worth of brown and proceeded to attempt to smoke it with a large rottweiler cross nudging and sniffing at me. Within ten minutes we were grouching and decided to go back to Weasel's flat and finish the rest. We had a great time. I think Weasel was doing this because of pressure to succeed whereas for me, well it washed away all the anxieties and pain. We returned every day for 9 days and Weasel paid for most of it. He'd turn up after work at about 4.00pm and pick me up – off we'd go.

Then Christmas Day arrived. Weasel had gone away and I had no money. I was getting increasingly ill and remember writhing in pools of sweat although I was still cold and shaking. I lay on the sofa, paced the floor, every illness at once. All I could think of was ending my sorry existence. Half past eight the following Boxing Day morning I managed to get a response from Animal. He'd help me. That was it – hooked on heroin!

Chapter 8

It's hard to believe now looking back over the years that Ben had managed up until this point to keep the seriousness of his habit from us. We knew he drank, sometimes to excess, we knew he took cannabis and that had got him into trouble with the police a couple of times but we had no idea how deep he had got into serious addiction. In those days, the early years of the new millennium, little was talked of drugs and we, his parents, were total innocents. We knew no-one who had the problem with their children, or if they did they certainly never talked of it, and Ben was very good at hiding things from us, sharing emotions and problems only when he wanted to. If Ben didn't want to talk or tell you couldn't get anything out of him. To be honest we'd put most of his problems down to some sort of psychiatric problem. When Ben tried to kill himself straight after Sarah's wedding day he was under a psychiatrist that we were paying for him to see privately. The psychiatrist had diagnosed a chemical imbalance but when Ben took all his medication in one go ending up in hospital for a stomach wash, called him "a silly boy", which distressed and infuriated Ben to the extent that he wouldn't go back again.

Steffi came up with a list of various help agencies and in desperation we asked Ben to look at the list and choose something or someone who he thought might be able to get him well. Ben chose a medical hypnotherapist who had a clinic the other side of Burton-on-Trent. We arranged for

Ben to go and see him. Ben went for three sessions over three weeks. The first time he came home he seemed glad that he'd been, although he told us nothing of what had transpired. The second time he was very subdued, but the third time he was totally distressed and refused to return again.

What these sessions had uncovered was the incident that Ben has touched on twice in his writings but it was a long time before Ben opened up to us what that incident was. I will relate it here as best I can. The incident came up one day when I had a fierce row with Ben and had to physically restrain him from getting out of the front door. We sat down together on the settee and Ben talked, unravelled a bit really, and one of the things he came out with was what the hypnotherapist had uncovered on that last visit. It was an abusive act that a friend of the family had committed on Ben when Ben was seven years old. He refused to tell me who it was, saying that it was in the past. You can imagine how this incomplete piece of information played on mine and Mike's minds. Who could it have been? We went through all our adult friends who were around us at that time but drew a complete blank. No one that we knew closely could or would have done such a thing. It must have been in Ben's imagination.

It was to be three or four years before Ben came out with the name of the perpetrator, who turned out to be a friend of Sam's. You will remember that when we moved to Alton, Sam was 12 years old and not happy with us uprooting him from his surroundings and his friends. In order to help Steffi and Sam settle in we had friends of them both coming for stays during the summer school holidays and it was one of Sam's friends that Ben named. If Ben was seven when the incident/s occurred then Sam's friend would have been 16. If you, M.B., ever read this book, shame on you! It was probably just a dirty little game you played with Ben but it was enough to ruin Ben's life. It certainly explained Ben's very low self-esteem from an early age despite having all the support and love a family could give around him. If only Ben had told us when it happened, it could all have been explained away to him. Instead I think he buried it into the back of his mind where it took root and festered. My poor little boy, you try so hard to protect your children, to do what is best for them but nothing is fool-proof. Ben was damaged and we had known nothing about it.

This is one of Ben's sketches and I think it illustrates perfectly his pain:

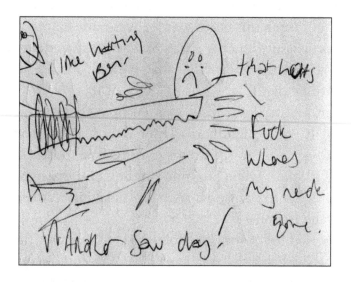

I like hurting Ben
That hurts
Fuck where's my neck gone
Another saw day!

Chapter 9

Ben was in his early twenties when he told his dad that he had a problem with drugs and that he was on heroin. They decided to tell me together. Ben probably needed his dad's support on this. He knew how calmly Mike dealt with everything whereas I was the exact opposite, and they told me together in the kitchen at home. Mike said, "Ben has something he wants to tell you." "What now," I probably thought. "Mum, I've got a problem, I'm on heroin and I want to get off," said Ben. Strangely enough I took the news very calmly but I think this was because I was quite ignorant about serious drug issues and my reaction was to say that we would help him, and that's exactly what we did, for the next 13 years until he died.

What followed was his first attempt at cold turkey under our roof. It was a nightmare. Three days it lasted before he ran off to get a fix to satisfy his craving. We took it in turns to stay with him, talking to him, holding him, sponging him, listening to him crying and begging and shaking. A nightmare, and not the last one.

A period of normality followed. I suppose Ben was managing his habit, he was working so he could pay for his drugs. He had met up with a girl, again one that he had gone to school with. Lynne had returned to the area from Preston where she had been living and contacted Ben. What Ben didn't know initially was that she also was an addict and needed a supplier. She'd heard about Ben's addiction and who better than to help her out. Addicts I feel are very needy, and tend to cling together. Initially, though, Ben couldn't believe his good luck. Lynne was gorgeous-looking and she was interested in him. He hid her addiction from us for most of the time they were together. She too got a job at the call centre in Derby where Ben was working and they held down their jobs for over a year.

Nothing stayed normal with Ben for long though and they decided they were going off to India together. It was to have been the holiday of a lifetime for both of them but I suspected it was also where drugs were cheapest and where they could indulge themselves to their hearts content.

Amongst Ben's belongings I found he had kept a journal of their time in India and Nepal and I was surprised at the normality of it. Apart from mentions of Valium and weed there is no record of heavy drug taking and he even talks of them getting clean. However, the last entry is when they landed back in England and it was '*got home with 20 grams of H – rear'*.

They left on the 3rd January 1997 and returned on the 22nd March. From his journal it was obvious that there were a lot of ups and downs. Lynne was quite a volatile personality, very moody and, according to Ben, not very demonstrative, so it was quite a surprise that when they reached Nepal towards the end of January they decided to get married. They were staying with a Nepalese family, cheaper I suppose than the hotels that they had stayed in, or maybe there are no available hotels in Nepal. They travelled to Sonauli on the Nepalese border on a train that got derailed at Gorakhpur, and ended up with this family who lived on a hill overlooking Phewa Lake. Ben was stressed because he couldn't phone us as the lines were down in Kathmandu and he sounded quite homesick. With the help of the Nepalese family, Lynne and Ben married on the 30th January in a Hindu Temple with the Himalayas as a backdrop. They were togged out in the traditional Nepalese clothing and there was a dancing party to follow. Ben wrote in a letter home to us:

*I am mentally strong and Lynne is a brick! She's made the last month a lot easier than if I'd been here alone. She has also helped me to stop and think before relapsing. I thank God every night for her and my second chance. Without you guys and Lynne I would not be alive today. We may have got married Hindu, BUT, I believe it does not matter which path you take – the end result is God. Personally I pray to Jesus. I prayed in the Church of England church in Shimla which is very much like England...*Ben loved India and Nepal, especially the Nepalese people. He was in awe of the sights and scenery and talked a lot in those early days back home about all that he had seen and experienced. I found this observation amongst his belongings, which I find quite touching:

Life and death is very ordinary in India. Death is accepted so readily that it's a scary concept for a westerner to accept. I put it down to the mass over-population – someone dies, the next generation needs feeding. They would probably tell you it was more to do with their religion and utter acceptance of it. Either way people are very quickly forgotten about there. People move on quickly. This makes me value my own life a bit more. If I went missing or got killed who, bar my family, would remember me? I'd made zero contribution to this life – maybe one day I could.

Wouldn't it be lovely if Ben's story ended here with a happy ending? Ben and Lynne back home, committed to spending their lives together as a couple. The euphoria didn't last long, however, thanks to their escalating habit, and to be honest I think Ben was relieved when Lynne exited the scene. Their rows were spectacular, though never violent. I would add here that Ben never lifted his hands to his dad or me. I was never afraid of Ben, he never threatened us physically even though I, I'm ashamed to say, lashed out at him.

The last time I saw Lynne she was having a terrible row at a local petrol station with her then-boyfriend, a drug dealer who was eventually sent down, but then, shortly after the Sky documentary went global, she rang me from Australia. Her mum had emigrated there a few years previously, freely admitting that it was to get away from her daughter, and now here was Lynne ringing me from down under. I'm happy to say though that Lynne is now married with two children. Her drug taking days are behind her and she now has a settled life. Marie, too, emigrated. She is living in Canada and is also married with two children and very content. I am happy for them both.

Chapter 10

There was a very elderly lady living in our village at this time and Ben used to cut her lawns. He was very friendly with her grandson who lived in a neighbouring village. This friend, Derek, was older than Ben and had a wife and children, but he also took heroin. Ben told me that Derek was desperate to get clean and had gone to the hospital unsuccessfully for help. He had then gone back home and hung himself in the garden. His wife had discovered what he'd done and he was cut down still breathing.

Derek lay in a coma for two years before he eventually died. Ben was terribly distressed but nothing changed for him. He continued to abuse himself, and it is abuse, but he abused us too in a way. As for help, in those days there was no help for us. We were trying to support Ben without any help whatsoever until one day a friend rang me. She had seen an article in her local newspaper about a drug support group that had opened up in Uttoxeter offering help for families of addicts. I rang and spoke to a young woman who said that, "Unfortunately you are not on my patch, however if you could get your friend to let you use her post code then I could take you on." There wasn't any help that covered my 'patch' so I lied. Sue was my lifeline and counselled me for some months. She also started a family support group which met in a church hall and there I met two other families who were struggling. One family had two sons and a son's girlfriend on drugs! How they managed I'll never know. The support didn't last long though, as the funding was withdrawn and the agency disbanded.

Towards the end of the nineties, help came in the guise of an old school friend of Ben's, Richard. The last time I had seen Richard was when Ben was in St George's Hospital in Stafford. He was in there for a detox when he in his early twenties and what a farce that was! Whilst he was there he could have visitors, anybody could visit, and during his stay he went out into Stafford for the afternoon with Richard and they both had piercings done! It came as no surprise when Ben failed a urine test and they kicked him out, but weren't they setting him up to fail by allowing visitors? When they told him to leave he begged for another chance but they were adamant and said he could apply again in six months. Richard was living in London in a very smart flat in Docklands and he had a job in Bond Street. He convinced us that he would sort Ben out. We visited Ben at Richard's and it was a lovely cube-shaped flat, with the lounge, shower room and kitchen in the bottom space and with stairs rising to the bedroom which over hung the lounge. Amazing design. It was deemed to be a luxury pad with a communal swimming pool and every morning Richard would either force Ben into the shower or into the swimming pool. I think Richard tried really hard with Ben but it destroyed their friendship. Richard was out at work all day so couldn't keep an eye on what Ben was up to when he was away from him.

Ben reckoned that Richard had loaned him his very expensive Tag Heuer watch and Ben said he'd been mugged. He even had the bruised ribs to prove it! Ben had obviously stolen it from his friend and sold it. Richard was furious and they came to blows. He kicked Ben out and who can blame him for that. We were called in to clean up his mess yet again.

We had a lifelong friend who lived in London and we called on him to see if he could help Ben get a job. Our friend came up trumps with a job as a runner at a film studio in Stratford. For Ben this was a dream job, and where he got his taste for camera work. He held the job down for two years and was absolutely devastated when he lost it. It was during his time at the studio when we paid for his first treatment at Detox 5 in Ealing.

Ben writes:

My dad and mum took me to the clinic although I was living and working in London at the time. I took two weeks off work at the film studios and went to my parents' house for a day or two beforehand. I'd bought a quarter a few days before I was due to go in, needless to say it disappeared pretty quick. It was to be a new start, I wanted it all over.

The staff at the clinic were nice but the nurse was unable to get blood from my collapsed veins so I asked for a 5ml pin and withdrew blood from my groin one more time. I was already getting sick. I'd taken all my junk the day before. I'd been kidding myself that I needn't save any for that day as I would be withdrawing by the time I got there. In truth a junkie cannot save gear, the more that is available determines the size of the habit but in truth I was pigging sick of the fucking stuff.

I have very few memories of my six days in the hospital. I was slipping in and out of consciousness, my dreams in and out of reality. During my stay in Ealing I had a small Ghanaian night nurse. She would sit with me to ensure I didn't choke on my vomit. I do recall trying to get her phone number off her and then promptly throwing up into her lap. On the fifth day I was introduced to the brain blockers – they helped with the cravings and would also make me very ill if I relapsed. I was terribly sick that week until I turned round and talked to my medication. Something along the lines of, "right you little bastard. I'm going to eat you up." After that burst of strength, the tablets no longer made me ill.

Ben returned home for a few days to recuperate…

It was strange being around my family that week. They'd endured so much over the years and yet they still believed in me. A lot of 'well done's' and 'I'm proud of you Ben' were said. I didn't know how to handle this at all. I explained myself by saying that I felt no self congratulations only sorry that it ever happened, simply it should never have happened.

I returned to work after a fortnight. "You look ever so well" exclaimed Jan. I pretended that I had been in France for the break. I was very much in control for the first month. The worst of it was not knowing what to do with my time. All my friends that I had anything to do with outside of work were involved with heroin. I spoke to one or two during those weeks, but soon realised that they hadn't anything to say for themselves. They just became people I bumped into occasionally and say 'hi' to, there was little else left to say.

I sometimes would bump into a couple I'd known during my last year on gear. I'd met them originally at Forest Gate overground station. TJ and I would ticket tout there. They were particularly into crack. I'd only gone a few weeks clean and I found myself buying crack with them. I think boredom and not feeling a part of anything at that time were the major factors in this. I made it clear that they were never to offer or tempt me with heroin and quite frankly I believe if they had any they wouldn't be offering. Crack is far more of a head fucker than brown. It doesn't have withdrawal systems like heroin but after one hit you would do pretty much most things to have the next.

I'd been paid and without a habit to feed found myself buying four quarters of the rock. As so many times before we happened to get a hanger on who, although he had no contacts of his own, had a brown habit. TJ would get his cheaper the more he bought. He took a oner off this fellow and we scored off P's little brother. You could tell the hanger on was sick already, mucus was running from his nose and he was shaking badly. "Where are we doing this TJ?" "There's a squat we've got near the station" he replied. Within ten minutes we were letting ourselves into squaller.

I was very edgy and nervous. I had a bad feeling. It would be just my fucking luck to get nicked now that I was clean. I don't know what made me worry about the others but I recall warning them all of the strength of P's gear. He sold scag straight from Pakistan. People have different resistances to junk, usually depending on (a) their finances and (b) how strong a drug their dealer was supplying them.

I made a pipe out of a discarded coke can and loaded myself a far too large pipe. By the time I'd loaded a pipe for Nicky, TJ's partner, the fourth guy had cooked up and was proceeding to bang up. He reassured me that he'd *only put half his quarter in. I knew instantly something was wrong. He was gouching before I could even inhale my stone. TJ ran out shouting "I'm going to get breached, jail for some fuck we don't know, don't be daft Nicki, don't be so fucking stupid Ben, for fucks sake you warned him". TJ ran away. I pulled this guy onto his back and got a scared Nicki to pump his chest whilst I inhaled and exhaled for this bastard. I told him.... I fucking told him. It took us to be point of defeat when he gave one of those last GASPS. They say you give them on death's door – one last cry into the cold, left to die without anyone caring enough to at least try to save your sorry frame. I saw myself as the same poor soul in the same state. He lived! I walked him around for an hour or so, holding him up and making sure he stayed awake. I felt good, a couple of months before I would have been the guy too scared to have tried and would have done a runner. Not needing the pressure, another nobody in another empty squat, another family not knowing for maybe months where their child was.*

We all have a tolerance but sometimes we don't see it. Sometimes our eyes are too big for our own good, sometimes we're just unfortunate. But the human spirit is a strange thing. You know when you're low and defeated and you know when you're elated, the first being the dangerous one. Anyhow I felt for once that I was here for a purpose, a reason. I can't say the feeling lasted but for those few hours I knew that if I'd died during one of my very many nine lives that I'd used and abused that I wouldn't have been in the right place to save someone's life. A little like James Stewart in 'It's a Wonderful Life'.

As I said before, the feeling doesn't last but for those few hours I was someone's hero. We are all ultimately responsible for our own existence but sometimes we need to be in the right place at the right time.

Chapter 11

I suppose the very worst job a drug addict can have is in a film studio where temptation is all around you, although probably more for cocaine and designer drugs than heroin, and Ben wasn't called the 'runner' for nothing. I know though that he did take his studio duties seriously, he loved being in the thick of it, able to meet and observe actors that he had admired and even getting a crowd scene part in a couple of films. Every night was party night, but it couldn't last forever.

Ben writes:

I was still working at the film studios, pampering all the folk with high class habits and no morals. I'd gone from Runner to Liaison Manager overnight. Blew my fucking mind. I'd been through Detox 5 and was clean. Money was 15 grand, should have been fuck ok but what came about was four months of complete chaos.

I used to get myself into all sorts of situations. I was drinking with a coke dealer who funnily enough was a carpenter. I imagined him snorting sawdust by mistake. Fuck that would be funny.

I couldn't believe the world I was mixing with. I was a fellow that made things happen. I had a sort of magnetic energy at this time. I could have become a leader; people were listening to me for the first time in my life. I was so good at acting, pretending. I thought it ironic that it was at the studios that it manifested itself.

How had I managed to suppress this magnetic quality that was opening doors and allowing me to behave in any manner that suited me. I'd use expressions like 'excess is not enough' often putting my words into action. Excess never knocked me down. Enthusiasm can only be fuelled by itself for so long, eventually you look for those substances that can help ignite and engulf the soul like onlookers can only drool at.

The film and media business is flooded with coke which I'm sure is mainly used as a designer accessory rather than a drug for performance.

I'd been at the studios now for 16 months and knew all the regular clients both socially and in business. I found myself in the position of going and buying a half gram of Charlie and Gary laying on me 5 grams. "Geezer, if you get rid you can get freebies all the time".

Ben stayed clean from heroin for two years and relapsed just weeks before meeting up with Emma again. Ben had known Emma since high school when they were both 13 years old and they had been in and out of each other's lives over the years. They connected again through Friends Reunited four years before Ben's death. Ben told me that he relapsed just two weeks before they met again. He was gutted. I'm not sure that the relapse happened because he was sacked from the studios or whether he had started using again and they had found out and got rid, but either way after managing to stay off heroin for two years he was back on it again.

Emma was working in Wolverhampton at the time and I think Ben managed to keep his problem from her for quite a while. He was again without a job, having been fired from the studios, and in serious trouble with the police. Ben was begging outside Bow Street Tube Station and was approached by a plain clothes policeman. I don't know exactly what happened but it ended with Ben up at court on a charge of common assault. He was fined £400 with £139 costs. No prizes for guessing who it fell upon to pay his fine.

Ben and Emma were totally in love and Ben made a real effort at this stage, managing to get himself a job as a process engineer with an engineering firm. I think he did quite well with the job initially and left of his own accord at the end. A couple he became very friendly with at this time came to his funeral and it was a total shock to them that Ben was an addict, they had had no idea.

Ben:
I was living in London and managing to hold down a job in engineering but eventually, due to my inability to cope with everyday problems, ended up living in my car whilst still working.

Emma moved to Bournemouth to start a new job towards the end of 2003, and Ben joined her, giving up his job so that they could be together. Emma still had no idea what she was letting herself in for.

I don't in all honesty think anyone tried harder than Emma did with Ben. Once she found out what he had been hiding from her she became determined that they would beat it together. She accompanied him to the doctor's, to hospital and to agencies, to try to get him quickly onto a detox programme. You would think that if an addict wants to come off heroin and go onto a substitute it would be a simple matter, but no, it's not, you have to wait, and with Ben it was a six month waiting list. Ben had acquired his first camcorder and started filming his story, with Emma interviewing him about the reasons for his addiction and what was he doing to help himself get clean.

Ben – taken from his film footage:

Hopefully tomorrow I get on the detox programme and medication. I want to go on DF's and not onto methadone. I think it will make the detox harder and I think it will be a slower process. Methadone is mainly for maintaining the habit and maintaining your health and is a ruse for keeping crime down rather than a cure, whereas DF is a codeine based pain killer. Last weekend I took ten over 60 hours which is the equivalent of 35mls of methadone but then when I went to try to get help on the Tuesday morning after the Bank holiday weekend the doctor wouldn't help me. So I have had to wait for my referral so three days of hard work for both of us, not just me going through this but Emma is going through hell too. Yesterday she had to look after me when I was poorly and that's a really difficult job. She wants the best for me and the best is to make me better. It is completely against her principles and fills me with shame. So hopefully tomorrow with a referral from my key worker in London, Kim, the doctor will assess me although I am not expecting to get prescribed DF's straight away but hopefully in a couple of days.

I am determined to stay well. I have to stay well and that involves taking heroin each day until I get onto the DF's. How much heroin I take depends on the quality and size and it'll cost £20 to £30. These last couple of days I am more scared, more ashamed, I have more anxiety and self loathing. I have not dealt with it very well. My stomach is dodgy, I'm panicky, don't sleep, get irrational, very scared, my nerve ends are shattered at the moment. I want it to be now. Emma doesn't have the luxury of knocking the pain out of her like I can – well I can for short periods of time – but Emma can't do that. This whole episode has brought us to the edge, right to the limit of our relationship but at the end of it we will be stronger. I know it's what I want. I know the next few days will take the hardest amount of personal effort I have probably put into anything. I know how much Emma means to me and how much I love her. I am not going to fail.

I don't know where Ben acquired the camcorder from but it went missing about six weeks before he died. He was always messing about with it, sometimes filming Mike and I as if he were interviewing us. I found it quite a nuisance and wasn't very compliant. Only much later did I discover that unbeknown to us he sometimes put it on a shelf and left it running.

Ben had another try of going down the cold turkey route here at home with us, and the row we had over that is well covered in the Sky documentary. Ben must have placed his camera on the kitchen table and left it running because I am filmed ranting and raving at an obviously stoned Ben, who had been driving his car under the influence of some substance or other. Strangely enough the camera isn't angled to show above my shoulders so I am headless – I could be any addict's mother giving their son the same argument. Any mother in the same situation would identify with me the frustration and anger I am experiencing when I say, "you know Ben, you give us a little bit of hope and then you snatch it away again."

Ben wanted to get some pot to help him detox, which I didn't agree with. To me it didn't make sense to detox whilst you were taking cannabis! I think he lasted about four days, during which time we succeeded in keeping him from escaping through any one of our four exit doors but we hadn't allowed for windows. Ben jumped out of his first floor bedroom window, breaking his foot on landing and running off to get what he needed/wanted. I hear you asking where he got his drugs from in a village of this size, but Ben never had to travel more than two miles to find cannabis and four miles to buy heroin and, of course, there is a delivery service if required.

Ben got quite paranoiac about security and was worried sick that the cottage would be broken into. He begged us to get a security alarm fitted and, in order to keep him happy, Mike painted a tin to look like an alarm and fitted it above the garage door. It was so realistic looking that Ben was able to relax a little.

To give Ben credit, though, we were never subjected to the dealers, although we did on several occasions drive him to a destination for collection. Mike being party to this is also shown in the Sky documentary and we have been criticised for doing this. I know it was wrong, I know what we were doing was breaking the law and it wasn't something we did without having lengthy wrangles with Ben. In our defence all I can say is no-one knows how they would react in the same desperate situation when your son is obviously in pain, crying and begging us to help him.

We offered to fund him again for detox. Ben said he was ready, that he had to get clean as his relationship depended on it. This time he applied to Detox 5 in Harrogate at a cost of £3000, as the price had gone up £1000 since his Ealing treatment. When we took him there in 2003 little did we know that Ben had less than three years to live. I wonder if he had known then what we know now, would it have helped him?

Ben wrote:*When I started taking smack it probably saved me from myself. I was on a mission of self destruct once again. I'd lost several people very close in quick succession. No excuses I know but junk meant I had to stop all reckless behaviour, all social life and more importantly it gave me what I hated most, a routine. I embraced the stuff for the first five years and despised it for the remaining three. I set off smoking but inevitably turned to injecting. When no visible veins were available, I turned to injecting into my femoral artery which runs through the groin and the leg and is the second largest artery after the jugular. Once you've found that, as long as the needle is long enough, you can continue re-using until either you lose your leg, testicles or get free, or, and this is always a very real possibility with this vein, you die.*

With the knowledge of the hospital on the horizon, instead of cutting down on my heroin input I started snowballing it with crack cocaine. Fucking crazy! I'd every opportunity to embrace the future but I never thought I'd be free until it actually happened. Plus it gave me a month or two of good old fashioned sadness, self pity – every smack head in the world would surely die if they had to deal with expectation, happiness and the thought of a successful future. Sadness does carry a certain comfort, sadness doesn't let you down.

Ben had got another job prior to detox, a driving job, but he had to take a week off in order to get detoxed. He lied to them about the need to be off work for a week by saying he had to go into hospital for a minor operation on his knee. He was by this time limping so it seemed quite plausible. Ben could not take any time off to recuperate after detox, which was absolutely stupid. Detox leaves you in a very weak state, emotionally and physically, but Ben couldn't be persuaded.

Ben wrote:

After five days, I came out of detox and had to start work immediately. Within a week I was driving the works van back from Birmingham to Bournemouth and fell asleep at the wheel. I was lucky to survive and that no one else was injured as I hit a lorry up the rear at a fast speed, writing off the works van and the job. I then relapsed due to a sense of complete failure that night and overdosed, but was saved by a paramedic. My health deteriorated very quickly and I ended up living rough and begging, depending on the kindness of church soup kitchens to survive. I had bad legs and a complete sense of defeat.

Chapter 12

Ben had not only lost his job but he had also lost Emma. In the run up to detox he had treated her very badly, even stealing some of her belongings to sell for drugs. Ben could barely walk, and couldn't put any pressure on one of his legs it was so painful, so he took himself off to the local hospital and they diagnosed deep vein thrombosis. I can't believe that after diagnosis he was allowed to go back onto the streets again to fend for himself and to treat the serious problem with self-administered heparin injections. At the time he was sleeping in his old car, which had no rear window due to a personal attack, and relying on a drop-in centre for showers and hot drinks.

Ben wrote:*Fortunately my parents never gave up on me. I never stole or hurt anyone intentionally except for myself that is. I was too much of a coward to end my life although the dark moments were very dark. It became clear that my relationship was finished and my parents came and collected me.*

That we could have left Ben in Bournemouth, sleeping in his car and coping with deep vein thrombosis, was never an option for Mike and me. I don't think we even discussed any alternatives. Ben had to come home and that is what happened. With hindsight, I realise that for Ben it was probably failure for him, back home living with his parents once again at the age of 32 with little to show for those years, and I remember saying resignedly to Mike at some point, "This is it, this is our lives from now on. Ben is always going to be with us, our lives will never be our own again."

Ben still looked good. He was handsome, looking younger than his years, except for his legs, which were awful to look at – very discoloured, almost black, and covered in a rash so irritating Ben used to scratch his legs until they bled. Apart from that, he appeared to be in reasonable health. He found it difficult to get a local doctor to take him on, but eventually a practice in Cheadle accepted him. It was the same with the dentist, as no practitioner really wants an addict on their books.

Ben also managed to get one final job which lasted three weeks. It was at the fairly new Toyota factory near to Derby. It was piece type work but he just couldn't keep up as his fingers were very swollen and stiff and rendered him clumsy. He never tried to find a job after this, concentrating his efforts on improving his benefits.

Drink also became an issue as he started to drink excessively, mainly cheap cider which he drank alongside heroin and diazepam. On drugs he was fairly docile becoming difficult only when he couldn't get what he wanted and the withdrawal pain and discomfort set in. With drink inside him he wasn't Ben – I suppose I could say I coped better with drugs than drink.

There were efforts made to get help for him during this time. He had a very good nurse attached to his doctor's surgery and she made arrangements for him to attend the Burton Addiction Centre, to which we were also invited. I know they do very good work there and get results but I have to say their approach was very wrong when we attended that day. It was a very small office and the chairs were arranged in a circle. As well as Ben, Mike and I there were four other people present. We all sat down and the session of questioning began. It totally freaked Ben out and he said he needed to go to the toilet. Looking back with hindsight, I can't believe they allowed him to go unaccompanied. We sat there for maybe ten minutes waiting for him to return and of course, he didn't! Ben had done what he always did best: run off. He never got another opportunity and the nurse who had tried hard to get him the right sort of help left the practice soon afterwards.

This then was the situation we had to live with these last two years: residing in a small respectable community with a son who had an obvious drink and drugs problem. I think the fight for recovery had gone from all three of us and it was now just a matter of survival. I love Ben, I loved him then and I love him now but I didn't like him or at least I didn't like what he had become. In those days it was difficult to remember the real Ben, the Ben that I had given birth to, the little boy that had brought us such joy, such pride. We had no pride left then, and I don't know how we got through those last few months.

Just over a year before Ben died he arrived home with a severe facial injury and a girl, Shirley, in tow. He had taken a real beating from her ex-squaddie, drug dealing boyfriend. Ben had witnessed her being knocked about by him and had brought her away at a cost. I was horrified by the whole situation and said she couldn't stay with us, whereby Ben said he couldn't leave her unprotected and if we wouldn't help then he would have to go as well. This led to the two of them sleeping rough on the outskirts of the village. In the daytime they were hanging around with a bin bag containing sleeping bags. Mike and I put up with this for two weeks and then told him to come back home and bring Shirley with him, but that on no account were we going to feed or look after them. A few nights later I had to take them to the hospital around midnight as Shirley was ill and was admitted with pneumonia.

Shirley remained under our roof for six months but very soon after she moved in Ben got into trouble again with the law and he was up at court in Burton-on-Trent for driving under the influence of drink. He was disqualified from driving and ordered to pay costs at £10 a fortnight. We knew nothing of this, and in order to try and keep it from us Ben bought every local paper from our newsagent and binned them, even though we hardly ever bought the local paper. No one else seemed able to tell us, however, and we remained in ignorance. If we had known what happened, the following month might have been avoided. He was stopped again, tested positive and banned from driving, this time for four years. He was also put on probation, "The best thing that happened to me for a long time," Ben said later. Ben never drove again but he never complained about it. He had passed his driving test first time when he was 17 years old, one of his very few achievements of which he and we could be proud.

To be brutally honest, those six months that Ben had Shirley in tow were the worst months of my life. Again we were kept in ignorance of her habit, which mirrored Ben's with the exception of alcohol: she wasn't a heavy drinker. She was a good ten years younger than Ben but looked as old, and, to be honest, she was a mess. If Ben had nothing else he had good manners and he knew how to hold a conversation. Shirley had no skills on this front at all. We were upset and angry that Ben had put us in this position, and it wasn't even that he loved her but I think that the one thing Ben was really scared about was being left on his own. When he lay down at night he had to have the television going in his bedroom. I would sneak in and switch it off once he'd dropped asleep, worried about the light flickering on his face all night, but it was on again when I got up the next morning.

There were several incidents whilst they were together, the worst one being when one evening Ben came into the kitchen to make something to eat. He had been perfectly alright minutes before but now he was unsteady on his feet, slurring his words but trying to act normal. He suddenly fell to the floor, striking his forehead on one of the large metal handles on the kitchen unit. There was blood everywhere. Ben was on warfarin for his deep vein thrombosis and that has the effect of thinning the blood, so there was no clotting and it just kept running and running. In the commotion that followed, Ben did what he always did, he ran from the house followed by Shirley. This was very upsetting for Mike, and I had to see that he was alright before I too went outside. I got my car out and proceeded to drive around the block and up the High Street, pulling up opposite our local village general stores. I didn't know what to do. My instincts were to keep quiet, maybe no one would see him in this state, but no, the door of the shop suddenly opened and out flew Shirley, followed closely by Ben. The lady that was working there that night also appeared and saw me standing over the road outside my car. She was rightly very cross. "Is that you Anne? You've got to do something with Ben but I'm telling you now, that girl is banned. I don't want the likes of her in this shop with the language she comes out with."

Ben's cut was a big one, and you could see his skull underneath. It continued to bleed, but not so dramatically. Ben would not let me take him to hospital to get it stitched and it was in that state when he went to probation the next morning. His probation officer took one look at him and sent him immediately to A & E.

Chapter 13

From then until he died Ben was in probation. Getting there and back wasn't easy for him, as it wasn't on a direct bus route and he had to go into Hanley in order to turn round and get on a bus to Blythe Bridge. He never once complained about the inconvenience, though: it was as if he knew he had got what he deserved and would get on with it.

As well as probation he was put on a methadone programme, which was monitored through the probation services. It meant they would test his urine to see if he had taken anything and he would see a doctor there from time to time. The methadone dosage starts at a high level and the aim is to get it down to 35ml when rehab will be offered, but to me this is a carrot dangling in front of a donkey's nose. It is almost impossible for an addict to get down to this level and at some point they usually relapse, take heroin then fail the next urine test, whereupon the dosage of methadone is raised right back up again. Soul-destroying.

Ben had been in probation for a month when his Dad became ill, and three months later we were told they couldn't find the primary cancer and that Mike was terminal. Ben asked Shirley to go back to her parents for Christmas so that we could have that time together as a family. We didn't ask him to do this, he did it of his own accord. Shirley went straight back to her old boyfriend, who incidentally had been put on probation for possession of a large quantity of heroin and other drugs It wasn't his first offence, and Ben and

Shirley thought he would get prison, but he got probation. He had to report to the same office as Ben, and on the same day. Ben was scared to go in case he ran into him and said he'd rather be sent to prison than get another beating, but probation were very good, understood the situation and let Ben move his session to another time.

I thought that whilst in probation Ben would be taught something useful, such as plastering a wall or decorating a room, but they look instead at what interests the offender and try to arrange it for them. With Ben, the first thing he put forward was poetry writing, so probation arranged for him to join a group. He kept this up for a few weeks and then said to me, "I can't cope, Mum, it's full of old ladies and all they want to do is read their poetry." Ben was very artistic so he thought he'd enjoy the 'box art'. Box art is creating an artistic scene in something akin to a shoebox. Ben wasn't happy with a shoebox, however, and wanted to create something that denoted homelessness, so he found the largest cardboard box he could find and took that along to the class. Using one of my lipsticks, along with other things, he wrote graffiti over the top and sides of the box. He draped an old sleeping bag in and outside and littered it with drink tins and cigarette ends. Still he wasn't satisfied. He acquired a fairly large mirror, set in the top half of a dresser, from someone in Cheadle and managed to persuade the bus driver to let him bring it home on public transport. This was to go in the back of the cardboard box and he wanted to project some of his film footage onto it.

I am positive that Ben's interest in film came about through his experiences at the film studios. He had also completed a computing course at Burton College learning how to create a web site a few months earlier, but he had no idea how to edit a small portion of his large amount of film footage to project onto the mirror to complete what he wanted to achieve. We couldn't help him, so he turned to his probation officer, Neil, for advice. Neil arranged for a young man, Darren Teale, from Junction 15, a small media company in Stoke-on-Trent, to come in and give Ben some help. Darren had done voluntary prison work before and he was happy to give his time to help Ben. Ben took his cassettes into probation for Darren to see and Darren was amazed. There was nearly 40 hours of footage. Darren was curious and asked if he could take the tapes with him to run through over the weekend to see what he'd got.

The next time they met, Darren told Ben that he thought there was a documentary in the footage and that they would work on it together and see what came about. They ended up with 'Sick and Tired of Feeling Sick and Tired', a 45-minute documentary that was very explicit and very harrowing. It did show Ben's humour, though, and when Sky made their documentary they unfortunately couldn't use the humorous content because it featured Sooty. Ben had a Sooty hand puppet from when he was a little boy and Sooty plays quite a large part in 'Sick and Tired' as a fellow heroin addict. Freud would have had a field day analysing this but I don't think Harry Corbett would have been happy. Funnily enough the Sooty puppet disappeared after Ben died, I couldn't find it anywhere.

Ben was so excited at this turn of events. It gave him something to think about and believe in. He was a mess by now. As well as drugs, drink was taking its toll, and he had totally lost his boyish good looks. He also knew his beloved dad was dying and this must have been a terrible thing for him to take on board. He had to get himself clean, now was the right time.

It would have been his 35th birthday that September, and as an early birthday present and an incentive to get detoxed we bought him a new camcorder. I am so glad I did, because without that we wouldn't have the footage he took the night before he went into hospital, two days before he died, when he expresses remorse and asks for forgiveness.

Benny Scisser Pants
oow! they hurt – honest

Chapter 14

Ben was desperate to get into hospital for a detox and the doctor attached to probation agreed that it was urgent. Despite this acknowledgment, there was a delay resulting in Ben begging and pleading, even breaking down at probation, for a bed in the detox unit at Stoke's Harpfields Hospital. That he had reached the end of the road was evident. He knew his body was caving in and, even more importantly to Ben, he knew his dad was dying and he wanted so much for his dad to be proud of him. That he loved Mike and I was never in any doubt although I remember saying to him once, "You have no father or mother Ben, heroin is your father and your mother." Ben didn't like that but that's how it seemed to me – that heroin came first.

The sixth of July was the date he was eventually given. He would be hospitalised for two weeks and I remember thinking, 'Thank God, we'll have two weeks peace, I'll be able to concentrate on Mike.' Then again the thought ran through my mind: 'will he stay in for two weeks or will he take off?' No matter; he was going into hospital, he wanted to go in, and he seemed determined to do it. With hindsight, and with the film tapes to verify it, I realise now how ill he was and yet he kept it from us as best he could. I'm wrecked when I think about how frightened and lonely he must have felt in those last weeks. When I am racked with guilt and feel I failed him, it's those last few months that I feel most guilty about. I was his mother, I had fought for him for so long, but at the end I think I gave up on him. He was in such a state those last few weeks – I never saw him take a bath, or a shower. He had totally lost interest in his appearance and yet Ben never smelt bad, with no body odour or bad breath, unless he'd been drinking, when you could smell the alcohol coming out of his pores the morning after. I also think that being on drugs must somehow have interfered with his physical development. He never needed to shave, even though he did occasionally try to encourage a beard.

The night before he was due to go into the Edward Myers centre, which is the part of the North Staffs Hospital complex that caters for those with addiction problems, he was very anxious and obviously under the influence of drugs. It wasn't drink – I could always differentiate between the two by the effect whatever he had taken had on him. He had to be at the hospital for 10.00 am the next morning and I drove him there. We talked quite positively and affectionately on the way there, a journey of about 35 minutes. He put his hand over mine on the steering wheel and said, "Mum you have lovely hands", which haunted me for many months after he died because all I could think of was the times I had lost it with him and lashed out.

He also talked about his documentary that he had been putting together with the help of Darren Teale of Junction 15, the media people called in by probation for this purpose. He was excited that it was nearly finished and was confident that it would make him rich and famous. He'd be able to pay us back for all the money he had begged, borrowed and stolen from us over the years. He would be very cross if he were here now, I believe, because Ben is still costing me money. I have made nothing from his footage, giving everything freely as has Darren from Junction 15.

"You know Mum, you are in the film," Ben told me reluctantly.

"Oh, am I, what am I doing?"

"Well Mum, you are shouting a bit." I don't think I do 'a bit'.

"And is dad in it too?" I asked.

"Oh yes, of course."

"And what's dad doing?"

"Dad's saying 'I love you Ben, I love you Ben.'" That was typical of how it was in our family; me doing all the shouting and telling off and Mike, my lovely, gentle Mike, confirming that whatever any of us did we were loved regardless.

I was there whilst they admitted him and hugged him when it was time for me to go. "I love you Mum, look after Dad," were his parting words. All the way home back to Mike I prayed that Ben would stick the course and not walk out on this opportunity to get clean. He had had a similar opportunity two years previously in the same centre, but that only lasted two days. Ben didn't want us to visit or contact him for at least three days, when he hoped he would be over the worst, but that night the phone rang and I knew it would be Ben even before I answered it. Thankfully he wasn't asking to come home, but that he was bored. He wanted to know if I could take in his favourite book on Everest, an achievement he much admired – he had many books on climbers who had achieved or failed the ascent. He also wanted some cigarettes – his resolve to give up smoking whilst he was in hadn't lasted long - and some soft drinks. I promised I'd take them first thing the following morning.

The next morning I got to the hospital about 10.30am and was dealt with by a male nurse who closely examined the bag that I was taking in for Ben, which was fair enough. I asked how he was and the nurse said, "Ben has had a really had a bad night and he had to be seen by the duty doctor." On asking if I could see him, this was denied but an approaching doctor intervened. He said that Ben had been really sick throughout the night but was sleeping now. "Can I not just look in on him?" I pleaded. The doctor told the nurse it would be alright for me to go as far as the door. On walking up the corridor I saw Ben's trainers sticking out of the doorway and I thought 'oh no, he's on the floor', but of course the shoes were just keeping the door open. He was in his bed sleeping and looked quite peaceful.

I so regret leaving him now – I should have insisted that I stay with him until he awoke, but detox units are not like hospitals; not so accommodating, and perhaps that's how it should be. When Ben was in St George's in Stafford, he was allowed unvetted visitors. Someone brought a substance in and Ben tested positive and was thrown out. Isn't that setting them up to fail?

I left the Edward Myers and drove round to get some paint from B & Q as one of the things I was going to do whilst Ben was in hospital was decorate his room. His bedroom was in a terrible state, especially as he had written on the walls snatches of songs and poetry, mainly bits from songs by the Libertines, and some desperate cries for help. I suppose I should be grateful that the 'decoration' was done with marker pens and not blood, as I understand other addicts have done. I then went on to Morrisons to do a quick shop before heading for home, and I got to the store about ten minutes to 12. It was the 7th July and exactly a year after the dreadful bombings on the underground and buses in London. I decided to observe the minute's silence in my car before getting what I needed.

I got home at 1.00pm just as the phone was ringing. Mike answered it first and he silently handed it to me. It was the Edward Myers to say, "There is no easy way to say this but Ben died at 12.30pm." Mike was shocked, and as ill as he was he said, "I'll drive."

"No, I will," I said, and as we were arguing about who should drive there was a knock at the door and David, who was a very good friend of Mike's, and had called in to see him almost every day throughout the time he was ill, said, "I'll drive."

Chapter 15

Ben,

It's all over. What we had dreaded for so many years had happened. Why Ben, why couldn't you have lived? I prayed so hard for you Ben when you were still with us. That the Lord would somehow miraculously touch you and turn your life around. It happened for one young man I was told about. John was a heroin addict living about seven miles from us and his habit caused him to steal, which resulted in him being sent to gaol several times. The stress of trying to cope with their son's addiction was instrumental in breaking up his parents' marriage. John got so low and so desperate that he turned to his family's church for help and a group of church people stayed with him for four days praying. Suffice to say John has got his life back. He is married, has a job working with youngsters and he now looks like David Beckham!

His Dad and I arranged for you to meet with John and you agreed but said it had to be in a pub not in a church. I don't know what really transpired at that meeting. When you got back home you seemed impressed at John's story but ultimately it had no lasting effect on you. I have wondered if you actually did turn up to meet John.

I don't know what your Dad and I could have done to save you more than we did. I know we could have done things differently but that would probably have meant turning our backs on you, refusing to have anything to do with you. A friend of mine did exactly that. It got to the stage with them that they couldn't keep on looking for their son who came and went as he pleased, turning up only when he was in trouble or in need of money. In the end they changed the locks on their doors. He is now a married man with children and holds down a very responsible job. I'm sure though that for every one that pulls through on their own there are many that end up dead like you, Ben.

So why weren't our prayers answered for you, Ben? I haven't got any answers but I do know that my God is good and gracious and it is not his will for us to suffer as we have suffered. My biggest fear was finding you dead behind your bedroom door as I had found you several times with the needle still in your hands, or that you would overdose in some dirty toilet somewhere as many do. My worst fear though was that you would die away from us and we would never know what had ultimately happened to you. So I thank God that you died in a hospital bed and that your Dad and I were very quickly by your side to witness that transformation in your looks. You were our boy again and the expression on your face was that of peace.

I prayed for time with your Dad, "just give me a couple of years," was my plea, but then that was not to be. Dad died just nine weeks after you. I do believe though that he had been given the strength those last few months because he didn't want to leave me alone to cope with you, Ben, but then when you unexpectedly died he was able to let go. His final words to us were "I love you," *and I know that you too were included in this. There was never any doubt that you were loved, Ben, but whereas my love was demanding and probably controlling, your Dad loved you unconditionally. He loved you despite the fact that you caused us so much worry and upset whereas I angsted and railed against it all the time. I always try to look for something positive and I suppose that if Dad had lived on longer then probably your film footage would have remained in a box in a cupboard, as I would have been concentrating on looking after him. I knew I had to forgive you Ben but not only that, I also needed to ask you to forgive me and I felt a peace after I consciously did this. This action of mine on forgiveness became very meaningful when we eventually saw the whole SKY documentary that was produced two years later.*

In those early weeks after you died, Ben, I worried about where you were. I know I kept saying it, sometimes out loud, "where are you Ben?" I suppose I needed some sort of confirmation that you were safe – that one day I would find you again, that you were not lost forever. That confirmation came when Olly brought the SKY documentary to our home the day before it was publicly screened for the first time at the Sheffield Documentary Film Festival. Dad and I had replaced your 'lost' camcorder just a few days before you went into detox. If we hadn't done that you would not have been able to leave the message that you did just the night before you went into hospital. These were the last words on the film footage -

"I think I'm dying …… if this is my time please Lord forgive me for all my sins. I have never been a bad person,

I never meant to be. I love you Mum, I love you Dad, I love my family. I'm sorry, sorry that I failed"

Thank you Ben and thank you God for the comfort that this has brought me.

Writing this book has enabled me to remember the young Ben that got lost over all those years of abuse. The happy, loving, cheeky boy that I gave birth to.

You had such a kind side to your nature Ben, and I can remember lots of incidences when this came to the fore. I remember when you were 15 and you had been to a village disco and arrived home with a young girl who was absolutely smashed and asked if she could stay with us that night as she dare not go home. I rang her Mum to reassure her that her daughter was in safe hands and she was.

I remember you arriving home unannounced when you lived away because you had heard that one of your friends had died. He had died because he had ingested a bag of heroin when the police came knocking at his parents door and the bag had burst. You had bought a bunch of flowers and went off to the cemetery in the village where your friend had lived to look for the grave.

At your funeral a friend of mine who lives in the High Street told me she always had very warm feelings for you. When they came to live in our village her daughter was in her early teens and had to get on the bus to travel to the High School where she knew no-one. You, Ben, had taken her under your wing, calling for her in the morning to travel with her and then sitting on the school bus with her on the way home, leaving her on her doorstep. It had given her the confidence she needed to face her new environment.

I need to hold onto memories such as these Ben, now that memories are all I have to cling to. When you were still alive the good times got lost because the bad things overtook all that had gone before. As Steffi said on the SKY documentary –

"there was lovely Ben and there was user Ben and there was an enormous tussle going on all the time. Ben, my brother, was like the rest of us – decent, a family man, liked to have a good laugh but he got lost in Ben the addict, and Ben the addict became twice as big as Ben the brother".

Ben with Sarah, Steffi and me

Ben and his Dad, Mike

LIFE AFTER DEATH

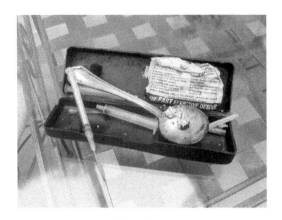

Ben's gear

Daily Mail report on the film footage

Chapter 1

I can't say we were surprised that Ben had died. It had always been

a reality for Mike and I, and we felt sure that we would live to bury him, but it was a shock happening as it did. After all, he had gone into detox to get well, not to die. When we got there the police were in attendance and, of course, asked questions, but we were dealt mainly with by a Mr Morgan, who treated us very kindly. I think Mike and I were both in shock as there were no tears, no disbelief, nothing just a horrible empty feeling.

Our youngest daughter, Sarah, and her husband, Phil, were soon by our sides and we were taken to see Ben. He was lying on his back with a sheet up to his shoulders. His arms were inside the sheet. A cold fan was blowing his hair and he had a gentle smile on his face. We all remarked on the smile and it has given me much comfort since, that in death he had found the peace that had so eluded him in life. It was also remarkable because when Ben was asleep, or under the influence of drugs or drink, his mouth sagged, making him look ugly. I hated that, I saw it much too often, but Ben in death looked like the boy we used to know before drugs aged and coarsened him. Ben was dead, he and we had lost the fight that had started 13 years previously when he told us he was on heroin and that he wanted to stop but he needed our help. For us as well as Ben the fight appeared to be over.

Chapter 2

Steffi writes:

I always knew Ben would die young. I believed for a long time that he could beat his addictions, and then I had a long period of time with a growing sense of desperation, helplessness and inevitability, where I knew his addictions had beaten him. Then, right at the end, I allowed myself to hope again because his whole attitude changed and he got his fight back. He was so determined to let Dad see him clean. When I got the phone call at work telling me he'd died, I ran into the staff room and overturned some chairs. I couldn't get my breath, couldn't remember which was my locker to get my bag, but inside, I had known this moment would come for a long time. Except I always thought it would have been through a fix going wrong, or an altercation with a dealer he had crossed; not in hospital through treatment to get him off everything. The irony of that was almost unbearable.

I was ten years old when my brother Ben was born. I remember the night he was born very clearly. My Dad had taken us to the library that day and I had borrowed a book called, 'The Green Book of Fairy Tales'. I had previously read the red and blue editions and was a confident and fluent reader, but the night my youngest brother was born Dad sat on the bed and read me the first story. The other two children were fast asleep and I loved having Dad all to myself as one story led into two. I remember feeling very safe and very secure.

Mum and Dad arrived home a few days later, along with presents for us from our new brother. I had some Pretty Polly hand lotion with a peach for the lid. I felt very grown up with three younger siblings to look after.

We were a big family with a lot of love to go round. I look back on my childhood and realise how very blessed we were. Our hobbies and interests were encouraged. We were listened to and made to feel we could take on the world and win if we were prepared to work hard for what we wanted. We were encouraged to be kind, to look at situations from another person's viewpoint and to look after each other. It was often noisy, brothers and sisters and friends everywhere, but we all knew we were loved and that we belonged. We were a family.

I left school and went to college where I qualified as a Nursery Nurse in 1980. I then moved away to a residential school near Cambridge and from then on I was no longer living with the family. Ben was, by now, eight years old. My memories of Ben from that time are precious. He was very slight in build, his hair often wouldn't lie down flat and he had the cheekiest smile. His beautiful brown eyes were vibrant and full of life.

It's strange, but looking back I don't really remember at what stage I became aware of a problem with Ben. I got married at 22 to Tony and we soon started a family of our own. Maybe I was too busy to notice, or maybe I was shielded from it. I do remember Ben drinking a lot at my sister's wedding and again that Christmas, but I probably put it down to him celebrating.

I do remember my parents telling me that Ben had told them he had been using drugs. I was confident that this was just a stage he was going through, that he had been reckless and stupid but he would grow out of it. I couldn't have been more wrong.

There then followed years of what my sister, Sarah, and I often referred to as 'Ben issues'. So many ugly memories of watching my little brother's life descending into total chaos. Not only was it painful to see Ben destroying himself, but there was the additional hurt of seeing my parents trying to deal with it.

I remember one occasion, Ben had seemed well for weeks and so, after a lot of thought, I asked him to babysit. I wanted him to know I believed in him, that I trusted him and I suggested the idea to Tony. He thought it was too big a responsibility, but as we were only going to a pub in the village with Sarah and her husband, Tony eventually agreed. Ben was happy to be asked and arrived early. The children were already asleep, and we left Ben sitting watching a video with a cup of tea. He told us not to worry and that he would be fine.

We were out for a couple of hours and then walked back round the corner to my house. Sarah and I were linking arms as we walked up the road and said how nice it had been to have a couple of child free hours. Tony and Phil were in good spirits chatting about the day's football scores. Then we arrived home. As we walked up the drive, I remember Tony saying that Ben hadn't closed the curtains properly and that anyone could look in.

We knocked at the door and there was no answer. We knocked again, and then again, louder this time. One of the children started to cry upstairs. Phil looked through the gap where the curtains weren't properly closed, and we could see Ben lying on the sofa. My initial, heart-stopping thought was that he was dead. He was lying face down on his front with one arm hanging down to the floor.

Another child started to cry upstairs. Tony and Phil were now hammering on the door and shouting through the letterbox, still Ben didn't move. I don't even remember how we got into the house but I remember a lot of shouting and then Tony shaking Ben awake. As Ben surfaced, obviously stoned and also quite drunk, I remember him asking Tony what all the fuss was about and laughing which incensed Tony. He didn't even know where he was, and I felt totally disgusted with him. I had trusted him and he had let me down, risking the safety of the children. Tony and Phil were both furious, and Tony was very angry with me for several days. The next day we discovered Ben had drunk wine and whisky from under our stairs and had also burnt a hole with a cigarette in the arm of our sofa. That was the end of Ben's babysitting career.

There were many incidents where Ben dominated everything. For years, I would ring my parents nightly and, until I heard their voices and knew everything was well, I had dull stomach pains. If they came on the phone and I could tell by their voices that there wasn't a problem, the stomach ache would disappear only to return the following night as I dialled their number. I was allowed to call Ben every name under the sun to my sister, but the minute Tony criticised him I would defend Ben to the hilt, which caused arguments.

One Christmas, Ben actually went into my sister's toilet and injected heroin with nine children and the rest of the family just a few feet away behind the bathroom door. My kids knew from a very early age that Uncle Ben was struggling with addictions and I was always truthful with them about it. It was impossible to keep it from them. They loved him very much and he in turn adored them. When my little boy Joseph died, Ben often visited the grave and told me that he would sit and have a chat with Joe. He also had his name tattooed on his arm which touched me greatly.

Family holidays, celebrations and day to day living were all impacted by Ben's addictions. I would buy him Christmas and birthday presents which I would never see again. I suspect they were sold to fund his habit. He only stole from me once, when he took three small bottles of wine in a wooden stand, a silver necklace and a building society card for an old and empty account. That made me sad. I would have given them to him if he'd been that desperate.

Towards the end, nothing Ben did shocked me anymore. He jumped out of a window when Mum and Dad were trying to help him go cold turkey and broke his foot. I was on my way to a concert that night, and nobody there would have guessed what I had left behind. Inside I had the stomach ache, the sense of foreboding, but over the years I had developed a place where I could deposit the Ben stuff deep inside of me, so that I could get through the days and be a good Mum and do my paid job as well as I could. When Mum told me she had found syringes and tinfoil hidden under the seat in her car, in the airing cupboard, under floorboards, I would cry and *worry and panic, then store the Ben stuff away and try my best to get on with day to day life. Sadly, Mum and Dad didn't have that option, and had to live with Ben's escalating problems at very close quarters.*

Ben was my youngest brother. For a long time after his death, I felt guilty. I had gone off the rails a bit as a teenager and wondered whether Ben had watched me and copied. Although I have never taken a drug in my life so I now think those feelings were probably unfounded. He infuriated me, and I hate that my parents were put through so much emotionally, financially and physically. I hate that my Dad never got a retirement due to Ben. I hate the fact that Ben's life and his future became smaller and less important than the heroin and I hate the way he died because it shouldn't have happened, but I never hated Ben.

I choose to remember the brother I used to push around in his large carriage pram, so proud to be his big sister. I choose to remember the brother who could make anything grow on a patch of land, garlic bulbs as big as onions and herbs that he would then cook in pasta. The brother who came to see me the night that my husband had collapsed and died, and, through his tears, said, "I don't know what the fuck to say," which was better than any platitude. The brother who adored cats and wildlife, mountains and music, poetry, Stoke City football club, stupid comedy programmes on Channel 4, the Libertines and his family.

At Ben's funeral, I had in my pocket some song lyrics from a song by the Welsh singer/songwriter Martyn Joseph, written by him and the poet Stewart Henderson. The lyrics included the line, "ambiguous answers, the question's still 'why', thunder and rainbows from the same sky," which to me sums up my brother's life. He had a huge capacity to love and to laugh and to keep trying, to never stop trying. The essence of Ben was overshadowed and often hidden by his addictions, but now I take great comfort in knowing that he is free from the hell he was in, free from his pain.

Chapter 3

We were in a dilemma. We didn't know what Ben would have wanted us to do with his body although we were pretty sure he would have wanted to be cremated. Two days after he died we had a visit from his ex-girlfriend, Emma. Ben only ever had three serious relationships in his adult life and they were all girls that he went to school with. He had known Emma since the first day he went to senior school when he was 12. Emma says she remembers clearly that first day in the new big school feeling lost and a bit overwhelmed when she saw Ben. Ben for her stood out in the crowd and they were in and out of each other's lives over the years, finally meeting up again about four years before Ben died. Two years previous to their reunion he had gone through detox and had managed to stay clean until two weeks before he met Emma again through Friends Reunited. I remember how distraught he was that he had met her shortly after relapsing.

Emma was able to fill in all the gaps for us when she came to see us that day. Yes, Ben wanted cremation, in a cardboard coffin, and he wanted his ashes scattering in the Himalayas. We said that this wasn't possible, and there was an alternative. Ben had also told Emma that he had a fondness for High Street, a peak in the Lake District that he had climbed once throughout the night with his brother, Sam, when they were living there. She even knew what music he wanted played at his funeral. Ben really had clearly sorted out what he wanted and it was all verified later when

I sorted through his belongings and found his wishes written down.

As Emma left, Iris, my ex-boss and great friend, arrived and obviously I told her what Emma had related to us. "The Himalayas are not an option," I said, only to be told by Iris that a party of boys from our local public school were going to the Himalayas during the school holidays. "Would they take Ben's ashes?" Iris asked. For obvious reasons I couldn't imagine them being able or willing to do that for Ben, and I certainly couldn't just ring up the school and present them with the request. However, through our church we did know one of their former school masters and I plucked up the courage to ring him to see if he could approach the school. Unbeknownst to Mike and I, he also couldn't imagine asking the school if the boys could take and scatter Ben's ashes, and he sought advice from our local vicar. Michael, our vicar, said he would pray about it and within a day or two ran into a lady from a village two miles away who was churchwarden at one of the other churches in Michael's benefice. In the course of their conversation she told Michael that her 19 year old son was travelling alone to the Himalayas in a month's time. Our vicar seized the opportunity and asked her if Olly, her son, would consider taking Ben. Her son agreed and, armed with a note of explanation from the undertaker, took one third of Ben's ashes with him, and I shall be eternally grateful to him for what he did. Accompanied by a guide, he trekked very near to the Chinese border, and the guide took photos of Olly scattering Ben's ashes. Upon his return from his adventurous holiday, he brought me photos and a map with the area in which he had scattered the ashes marked in red. Imagine our joy when Sam, our eldest son, identified the area as the trek he, his wife Jayne, and Ben had walked years previously.

Ben had had his wish, to be scattered in the Himalayas. The cardboard coffin was a little unusual but could be arranged, costing almost as much as a wooden one!

I have asked Sam to recall something of that trip to India when Ben was invited to join them and this is what he has written:

The last time I saw Ben before Jayne and I went to India was the day after he had been admitted into Cheddleton's psychiatric unit. Ben had scratched a cross into his forehead.

During our early months travelling in India, we received letters from Mum and Dad saying that Ben was doing well and looking forward to coming out and meeting up with us. I do, however, remember the feeling of apprehension as Jayne and I went to meet him at the airport outside Delhi. My fears seemed unfounded as he looked great.

Jayne wrote in her diary, "Ben arrived on time okay. It's great to see him and he looks very well." The next day she wrote, "Ben seems to really like it here although it must be difficult to fly straight into this heat and be jet lagged too. I think he felt a bit wobbly last night. He met a guy called Nick on the plane and they been off doing their own thing today, which is great. It's lovely to have him here – he's all smiley, which is good to see."

We stayed in Delhi for a couple of days and then took a train north to Pathankot as we were making for Rishikesh first and then on to Gangotri (the source of the Ganges).

Jayne slept on the train and Ben and I had a long chat. I remember that it was a difficult conversation. Ben was not making a lot of sense (to me) although to him he obviously was. He kept saying that God had spoken to him but, rather than sounding joyful or enlightened, he came across as irrational. After he had dropped off into sleep I looked out of the window for a long time. I felt depressed and helpless in that it seemed to me that he was still troubled and I didn't know what I could do to help him.

However, this feeling passed and during our time together there were many happy times. More often than not, Ben was good company. He socialised easily with others and made his own friends. He was often the butt of our gentle teasing. We were staying in a small place called Nagar in the hills outside Manali. Ben, who was in rude health up until this point, got sick and complained about coughing up three pints of blood! This tendency to exaggerate anything to do with his health always made us laugh.

In the Kulla valley, as in many places in the Himalayan foothills, cannabis grows as a noxious weed. You see it growing in massive thickets by the roadside. Ben was smoking cannabis regularly, though not excessively. Jayne and I, perhaps naively, didn't think this was causing him problems as he was still being sociable and was able to function well.

There were only two times when he was difficult to manage, and both of these involved alcohol. On each of these occasions he had found himself without cannabis and resorted to drink. When drunk, Ben would be full of self-loathing and self-pity in equal measure. To put up barriers, he would say what he thought you would want to hear. These were the worst times and he was always very apologetic afterwards.

My favourite times in India with Ben involved numerous bus journeys in the mountains. Whenever possible we would ride on the roof of the buses waving at people as we passed, being terrified at the views down into the valleys as the buses clung to the hillside and laughing. On one occasion Ben got horribly sunburnt. We still laughed at him and Ben laughed too.

When we returned to England, Jayne and I moved to Lancaster and didn't see Ben for some time.

Living in New Zealand, I didn't witness the last year of Ben's life. Mum and Dad protected me from the reality of it as best they could. When Mum phoned me and told me what had happened, it was a shock but not a surprise. Although nothing prepares you for that moment, I think that we had all lived for a long time with the possibility of Ben dying young.

I took Dad to see Ben in the Chapel of Rest. Dad wanted to go and I wanted to go to be with Dad. It was so sad. I was struck by now big Ben's hands seemed. I can't remember if I said anything to him. I left Dad to have some time alone with Ben and went and sat outside. I heard Dad crying and asking Ben for his forgiveness. I thanked the funeral directors for doing all that they had done.

When Dad died nine weeks later we were with him and it was beautiful because our last words together were an affirmation of the love we had shared. This was not so with Ben. I have many memories regarding my brother. As time has moved on, I have held on to the good memories and let the others go. The one real sadness that remains and that I still struggle with is that Ben died alone and I didn't get to tell him that I loved him.

Chapter 4

What really concerned me, though, was that I didn't think many people would come to his funeral. Most of his local friends had long since gone, either from the area or just from his life, and I thought they wouldn't have wanted to know him anyway, alive or dead. I was so wrong. First of all were the cards and letters we received, over 200. We were overwhelmed, and what I thought would be a half empty church was very nearly full and most of them were there for Ben, including officers from probation who had brought with them friends Ben had made in the twelve months since he'd started going. I was greatly touched by some of the letters and cards we received from probation officers, but even more so by those from some of his co-probationers. These are extracts from these letters:*"It was a pleasure knowing him, he was one of the most considerate and kind hearted person we have known, he used to cheer me and Sally up no end when we was down, he was so funny at times. Me and Sally have lived with drug addiction for so many years and know how hard it has been for our family too. We have now been clean off drugs since March and though Ben himself was waiting to go in hospital he said the kindest things to us and supported us. Where some people are jealous and nasty we are moving on Ben was genuinely happy for us and we will never forget that."*

"He was liked by everybody and he was one of the cleverest people I've met and had so many good ideas and good advice. I only knew him for almost a year

but he was a true friend with a heart of gold, one of the funniest and cleverest people I've met. He genuinely cared for other people. I'm so happy and proud to have known him (thank you Ben) and I know you must have both been so proud of Ben. I've never seen so many people at a funeral, just showed how many people's hearts he has touched."

"I only knew Ben for about three months but in those three short months Ben and I forged a very good friendship and he made my Monday afternoons so much more bearable and after a couple of weeks even enjoyable... I feel like giving up on life but I'm not, because I know it's not what Ben would have wanted...I'm glad Ben's at rest in heaven for three very good reasons I think. One, I know Ben won't be feeling any more pain or hurt and that he is at peace now. Two, I know Ben will be looking after my baby daughter who died two years ago for me. And three, I also have a younger brother aged 15 who is dying from cancer and, God forgive me for saying this, if he does pass away then there honestly would be no-one I'd rather have to look out for my brother than Ben.

*I have watched Ben's video diary and think it could make a big difference in a lot of young people's lives and I know that's what Ben was about. If it saves just one young person from the life that people like me and Ben lived then I know Ben has done what he has set out to do."*And from Neil, his probation officer:

*"Gentle Ben, never a dull moment! Your constant enthusiasm for everything you got involved with will be sadly missed, your creativity genuine and individual. Your time with us was a pleasure."*What we didn't want at the service was a cover up, for Ben's eulogy

to portray him as having led a flawless life with no mention of what had taken him from us at such an early age. My son-in-law, Phil, delivered the family's reflection – Phil has become the family eulogy deliverer having had to do Tony's, Ben's and Mike's. He'll be pleased to know I'll be letting him off mine!

This was some of that eulogy:

Ben laboured under a misconception for a great deal of his all too short life. You see, Ben thought that he only touched people's lives in a negative way. In this he was truly wrong. Ben touched many people in many different ways. He wasn't a saint by any stretch of the imagination, but he did underestimate his worth, both as a person and as a human being.

How, you may ask, do I know this? I see it reflected in the faces of the people here today. I have read it in the sea of cards that have taken up every surface in Anne and Mike's home and in the words that these cards contain. These next words are not mine, they were written by some of the people who were touched by Ben and whose lives he enriched.

"I greatly valued Ben as a friend, whose radiant smile in the good times would light up anybody's life."

"Ben had recently helped me out of a period of darkness. No matter how poorly he was feeling himself, he always found the time to say things that made me feel alive and happy again."

"Ben was a deep, loving and caring person."Ben was not a saint. For all too many of his years he battled against addictions to both drink and drugs. He was an addict, a fact that Ben never ran away from, he was very

aware of that fact and of the impact that it had on the people that he loved. He would not thank me if I did not acknowledge this; indeed he would be angry with me if I didn't. Ben would not want me to stand before you all and extol him as a paragon of virtue, so I won't!

Ben was an addict, that fact is plain, but he was also so much more than that. He was complex, sometimes infuriating, loving, gentle, stupid, wise, lazy, driven, giving, taking, a host of contradictions in fact, but then again aren't we all? What you saw wasn't always was you got. He was just Ben and knowing him you couldn't help but love him...Over the last four weeks of his life Ben and his Dad had been avidly following the World Cup, often watching three games a day and discussing the games and the merits of the various teams well into the night. It is a bitter irony that Ben didn't get to see the final. As his dad said, Ben was unfortunately 'sent off' before that came to be.

Ben packed a lot into his 34 years and experienced many things. I think that he was only truly happy a few times in the latter part of his life. I know for a fact though that during the time he spent travelling through India and Nepal Ben experienced a true state of spiritual peace and tranquillity. He loved everything about the place, especially the mountains. His whole being came to life when he described the grandeur and beauty of the Himalayas and he would become frustrated when he couldn't find the words to convey the wonder that he had felt to the rest of us.

Ben was climbing his own mountain, his own Everest, at the time of his death and it breaks my heart

that his body gave out on him just as he was preparing
for his assault on the summit…Ben never gave up on the
people that he loved, and they never gave up on him,
and I am so pleased that was the case. He left little of
material worth, but he left a legacy for his nine nephews
and nieces. He desperately did not want any of them
to follow the path that he had trodden. He constantly
warned them of the dangers of drink and drugs and
the impact that they had on his life. Ben's addictions
ultimately robbed him of many years of life and I know
that he would not want any of his beloved nieces and
nephews to fall foul of the temptations that ultimately
killed him.

Phil finished with the words:
>*"I believe in the sun even when it is not shining*
>*I believe in love even when I don't feel it*
>*I believe in God even when he is silent."*

Thank you, Phil.

On the back of the service sheet we printed one of Ben's
poems, written when he was part of the Poetry class that
Probation sent him to:

Heaven

I'm trying to be me
Or just trying to be
Humanity!
I'm kicking down doors –
Doors that are usually locked
Now they're not.
I'm crying tears, they disappear

Leaving the fear,
But no-one stays near.
I've found a belief, a belief and relief
That I don't have to achieve
There's nothing beneath
God gave us this peace
28.1.2006

We left the church following Ben in his cardboard coffin to the Lemonheads singing "I know a place where I can go when I'm alone" and then at the crematorium we left him there to, no prizes for guessing this one, Pete Doherty singing "When the lights go out, I no longer hear the music." Just as he wanted.

Sarah remembers:
Ben died in the middle of a heat wave, and the day of his funeral was beautifully hot and sunny. We all gathered at the cottage, Steffi and her children along with Phil and I with our children, and we were so pleased that Sam had made the journey back home from New Zealand. When Mum rang Sam to tell him Ben had died, his immediate reaction was that he wanted to come back for the funeral but Dad was adamant that Sam should not come back, saying that he refused to say goodbye to both of his boys that week. Thankfully Sam stood his ground and got back to Alton a few days before the funeral.

It's hard to describe our mood that morning. We were still trying to come to terms with Ben's loss. We were all aware of how frail Dad was and we were determined that Ben's funeral would be true to who he was and had been. We'd spent days choosing the right hymns and passages and were so pleased that Mum had found writings from Ben telling her what music he would want if this ever happened. We had all smiled when Mum read the lyrics to 'When the Lights Go Out' and said, "Will Pete Doherty do for Alton Church do you think?" Phil had spent hours writing Ben's eulogy, desperate to get the essence of Ben right.

Now we were ready and we didn't have a clue what to expect. Would we be the only people there to say goodbye? The funeral car arrived with Ben in the cardboard coffin he had also written about, and we walked behind the hearse to the church, which is just around the corner from the cottage. Dad was able to walk there with the help of Mum and a walking stick, the first sign of the incredible strength and determination he showed that day.

At the church Ben's coffin was put on a trolley – being cardboard we were unable to carry it, and the vicar came to meet us. Mum asked the vicar if many people were there and he commented that it was "standing room only." As we walked inside we were amazed and touched to see that the church was full. The service was lovely, Sam read from Psalm 103 and Phil delivered his eulogy with great dignity. We left the church to Ben's choice of the Lemonheads 'I Know a Place where I can go when I'm Alone'. Mum had decided that Pete Doherty was more suited to the crematorium! Once the church service was over the plan was for people to go to our local pub, The Wild Duck, whilst we went on to the crematorium. The crematorium is in Stafford some 40 minutes' drive away, and Mum's worry was that as we would be gone *for quite some while everybody would drift away. It was very endearing seeing her asking people to go to the pub, including members of his AA group!*

I don't actually remember much about the service in Stafford but I do remember that Mum was so overcome at the end of the service she was physically unable to stand up. We were sat behind her and it was Dad who held her until she was ready to leave Ben. It was to be the last time I saw Dad strong enough to look after Mum.

Once back in Alton we were touched to find that many people had stayed to see us and we met so many people that afternoon, friends of Ben from school through to new friends he'd made in probation. It was such a sad day, but it was also the first day that as a family we were able to start to talk truthfully about Ben's addictions.

Chapter 5

That Ben died before Mike was surreal, and to be honest I don't believe that I mourned Ben in the nine weeks after his death leading up to losing Mike. I think that to some extent Mike had hung on to his life because he was worried about how I would manage Ben with him gone. With Ben dying first, Mike was able to let go. It would have been Ben's 35th birthday on the 15th September and Mike was able to accompany the family to bury another third of Ben's ashes in the grave that held the remains of his baby nephew, Steffi's son Joe, who died of cot death when he was six months old, and the ashes of Joe's dad, my son in law, Tony. When Joe died we reserved the plot next to where he lies and that's where Mike is buried. I have my four men at rest together.

Mike died ten days later, and the day after Sam and I took the last of Ben's ashes to the Lake District and walked a little way up High Street, the peak that overlooks Haweswater, before scattering them. So Ben got all that he had asked for – no, that sounds all wrong. Ben didn't aspire to be a drug addict when he grew up, nor did he have a death wish, but I certainly think he knew he was playing Russian roulette and that sooner or later the bullet wouldn't be a blank.

Sam had to return to New Zealand the day after we went up to Haweswater, and as I sat there that evening I was overwhelmed with grief. "This is my life from now on, no Mike, no Ben – please God help me, I can't do this." I am by nature a practical person, however, and not one to ever feel sorry for myself, so I pulled myself together and looked around for something to do. "I know, I'll sort out the post," I said. I keep all the post in my hall underneath the hall table and the current post is stacked on top of a wicker basket, where I put the mail that I don't want to throw away just in case it comes in handy. I quickly sorted out the current mail and hesitated about opening the wicker basket, but I gritted my teeth and determined to get rid of the rubbish. Halfway down the basket the phone rang – it was Sarah, and we talked for probably an hour. When I eventually came off the phone I was drained and looked at the mess in front of me and the half empty/half full wicker basket. I briefly considered abandoning the rest but decided I would finish the task in hand and proceeded to do so, and I am so thankful I did. The very last piece of paper in the box was an A4 note from Mike.

Mike had to travel abroad quite a bit with his job and he always left me notes, always. I don't know when he wrote this particular one but I had kept it and it was amazing that I should find it the day Sam left when I was feeling so bereft. He starts the note by expressing his love for me and for his family and about how blessed we are. He says we will see this awful time through and wishes he didn't feel so helpless. He then goes on to emphasise five bullet points of practicality – where the candles and matches are, keep the phone charged, lock the door and put the electric blanket on early! But what sprang out at me was what he wrote at the bottom in large capital letters – IT WILL GET BETTER … I PROMISE. I have held on to that promise in my heart ever since – it will get better, Mike has promised me.

No one can prepare you for grief, and with hindsight I realise that my grief was not only confused but selfish. Some days I would be consumed by it and in my head I would wonder who I was grieving for, whether it was Mike or Ben. It was hard to separate the two in my head, yet I felt I needed to concentrate on one or the other. I don't know when my daughters grieved; they certainly did their best to keep it from me, and concentrated their energy on helping me to cope. I certainly was unaware of their grief, as after all I was the one who had lost a son and a husband. Only much later did the reality hit me that they had lost a father and a brother.

Two weeks after Ben died, Darren Teale from Junction 15 asked if he and his partner, Andrew, could come and see us about the film they had helped Ben put together through probation, the 'Sick and Tired' documentary. When Ben went into hospital for the detox, the film was more or less complete, with only things like music and titles to add and the plan had been that Darren would visit Ben in hospital with a contract that would give Junction 15 the copyright enabling them to get it out into the public domain. I'm not sure that Ben would have agreed to them having the copyright. He had spoken to me about the 'lads' saying, "They're okay, they know what they are doing, but I don't trust them." You have to remember that one of the side effects of taking drugs is paranoia, and Ben had that by the bucket load.

I liked both lads very early into the visit. They were only in their mid-twenties and I sensed their concern at having to show us Ben's documentary. I don't know how we got through that first viewing of 'Sick and Tired'. Although we were fully aware of Ben's lifestyle and the drugs usage, it's a very different matter when you are confronted with the reality of him preparing his hit and injecting into his groin. I felt physically sick and my first reaction was to think that no one must ever see it. Although, as a family, we had been relatively open about Ben's problems over the years, this was different – we would be exposing our shame to friends and strangers alike.

We talked at length with Darren and Andrew and from the documentary it was obvious that Ben wanted to get his story out as a warning to others not to get into drugs in the first place and where it could lead. It was also all that Ben had left to show meaning to his life. Darren said he thought he stood a good chance that Channel 4 would be interested and Mike and I agreed to sign the copyright over to Junction 15 – proof positive of the trust I felt in them.

Mike was very distressed when they had left. He was a very private man and although I have already said that we were very open about Ben's drug taking we didn't go around broadcasting the fact to all and sundry. Mike had continued working in the pottery industry almost right up to the end of his life, and he was worried that our private life would be exposed through the media of television. Nevertheless we felt we had done the right thing. Ben had left something very unique, nearly 40 hours of film footage, and to our knowledge no addict had ever done that before and, more importantly, it was really the last thing we could do for Ben. There was no doubt in our minds that that was what Ben wanted – he wanted others to learn from his dreadful mistake.

Channel 4, however, couldn't use it. They had been working on their own documentary for almost a year called 'Mum, Heroin and Me' so they turned Junction 15 down. I have to admit that my reaction to this was relief rather than disappointment. I had been spared the ordeal of anyone and everyone being able to witness what had gone on behind our closed doors.

Chapter 6

The inquest into Ben's death was called for Thursday, 23rd November, and I attended with my youngest daughter, Sarah. I was worried in case there was unwelcome newspaper interest but in actual fact apart from Sarah and I only the Deputy Coroner and his clerk were in attendance. At the time I thought I shouldn't be surprised, heroin addicts are perceived as scum and their deaths deserved, but that if Ben had been an Ecstasy victim that would have been so different, possibly a Grade A student and the only time he'd ever taken it. Drugs are drugs, aren't they, and I know that Ben took Ecstasy in his time and for him one thing led to another.

Mr Curzon, the deputy Coroner, was kindness itself, going through all the findings of the post mortem very carefully with us. He had underlined with pencil some of the things he thought needed highlighting and on request kindly gave me a copy of the report to keep. The exact wording on Ben's death certificate was:

Cause of death –
I. *right intracerebellar haemorrhage extending into brainstem*
II. *Supervised withdrawal treatment for drug abuse*

Verdict : The deceased died as a result of a recognised complication of drug withdrawal treatment.

When we left the court Sarah was visibly upset and angry. I have to say that Sarah is the most placid and even-tempered of my children, very like her dad in that respect. It takes a lot to make her angry. "Mum, there are so many unanswered questions. I do believe that the coroner wasn't satisfied with what he was delivering."I pored over the post mortem and toxicology reports when I got home, finally writing to Mr Morgan at the Edward Myers Centre on the 12th December asking for an opportunity to meet with him to discuss one or two vagaries that I needed to sort out in my own mind. Mr Morgan responded with an appointment for the 16th January 2007. I had many questions to ask, and Mr Morgan listened, but he made little in the way of notes, nor did he have any file on Ben or access to any computer. The questions I asked were:

Ben's cause of death was 'supervised withdrawal treatment for drug abuse – a recognised complication of drug withdrawal treatment.'

Therefore am I correct in understanding that the haemorrhage that Ben died of was caused by the treatment administered?

Ben was admitted for alcohol abuse. He was also on a methadone programme for drug withdrawal. *Was methadone administered in the 28 hours he was in your care?*

For the past two years plus, Ben had suffered from deep vein thrombosis. The last INR blood test was on the 15th June. *Was this condition taken into account before his treatment of withdrawal was started? If not, why not?* The coroner's report said that warfarin may have played a major part in the bleed to Ben's brain.

The drug administered was prochlorperazine which I understand is given for nausea and vomiting, which Ben suffered from badly throughout the night of the 6th/7th. On looking further into this drug, I understand that this should not be prescribed where there is a problem with liver function. The post mortem confirmed that the condition Ben had was steatosis, or fatty liver, recognised with alcohol misuse but which can be a temporary condition that clears when alcohol abuse stops. I know that Ben was led to believe that he had cirrhosis by the doctor treating him at probation and that this frightened him.

His left ventricle shows hypertrophy, which I understand is generally due to high blood pressure, something Ben never suffered from as confirmed by his GP. If withdrawal can and did make it rise from normal 111/83 mmHg on arrival to 170/96mmHg on the evening of the date of admittance, what was done to counteract this? I understand Ben had a really bad night, necessitating the duty doctor being called to him. The next morning he stumbled and fell, hitting his head against the wall, a fact I was told by the coroner not by the hospital. He complained of a headache, was seen again by the doctor who confirmed his high blood pressure, was prescribed two paracetamol and instructions were given to monitor him. *How do you monitor or treat for blood pressure?* My son had died alone less than two hours after I was allowed to look at him from the door of his room.

I was told at the time of my son's death that resuscitation is given by the ambulance station, although this was refuted by Mr Morgan at our interview. *Would they confirm that there are facilities for resuscitation in the hospital unit? If death is a recognised result of drug withdrawal treatment, then surely resuscitation is a must as should be close monitoring.*

Mr Morgan said my concerns would be taken seriously and I would be hearing from the hospital. On the 11th April I had to write to Mr Morgan again, some four months from my first contact, having received no response to my questions, sending a copy at the same time to the Chief Executive of the North Staffordshire Combined Healthcare Trust. I received the results of the review of my son's care on the 28th June and have to be content with their findings and assurance that lessons have been learnt from my complaint. However, my complaint had taken five months to be dealt with and then only dealt with because I had persisted in getting answers. I was distressed that Ben had been seen and treated as just an addict. He went into the hospital seriously ill and the documentary film that Sky made some time later verified that fact. The hospital had failed to recognise that.

Chapter 7

I became determined that Ben's film 'Sick and Tired' should not go to waste. It had a message and it was a message that I needed to get out. I had three aims for the film; first I wanted to educate the police and other authorities that there is another side to drugs, namely the victim's side, and the impact the addiction has on their families, secondly to educate the public that addicts are not the lowlife they are perceived as being and that for whatever reason they take drugs in the first place it very quickly becomes an illness and the drug medicine, and thirdly I wanted to get the message out to young people that if you mess about with drugs at best it will ruin your looks and mess up your mental health, and that at worst it could kill you.

I talked it through with my family as to whether or not I should proceed with the DVD, and they agreed unanimously that something good and positive could come out of Ben's life and our witnessing of it. We all had contacts with education, drugs agency staff and prison volunteers so I asked Darren if he could run some copy DVDs off for me. This he did, and I circulated them to Werrington Young Offenders, ADSIS, the AA, and one copy to my vicar, who took it to Ireland to a drugs worker he was in contact with there. All to no avail, as no-one fed anything back to me. No one out there with any authority seemed to be in the least bit interested!

No one that is except Mary Fox. Mary at that time was a BBC journalist working with Radio Stoke, and I saw her most Sundays at church. On talking to her about my frustrations, she pointed out that Staffordshire Police were very much in the news at the time as they were targeting drug dealers with dawn raids and arrests. They were calling it 'Operation Nemesis'. When Ben was alive it seemed to me that the police only ever arrested users like him. I used to wonder at the fact that, although they had followed Ben a couple of times after he had made his connection, they never caught the dealer at it!

Spurred on by Mary, I wrote to the Chief Superintendent who responded quickly, arranging for me to go to the station with a copy of 'Sick and Tired' to speak to a Superintendent, Mick Harrison. This I did early in October with some trepidation. I was going to say that it was my first time in a police station but I remember one other occasion when Ben was in trouble whilst still at school. He had got into a fight with another boy on the school premises. His parents pushed it to the extreme and Ben ended up in juvenile court. I soon relaxed though when we discovered that I was a friend of Mick Harrison's uncle and that Mick, like Sam, had lived in New Zealand. He took the DVD from me and said, "I can categorically promise you that I am going to show this to all my officers involved in the Nemesis drugs raids so that they can see the other side of the problem." This he did – it was seen by 400 police officers. I was thrilled. He also said he was moving shortly but introduced me to another police officer who would update me on any development with Ben's DVD and who I could contact if I needed to.

I felt I had to move on with my life and had booked a six week stay with Sam, and his family in New Zealand, travelling out on Monday, 29th October. I would take my eldest grandchild with me, Abigail, and we would go via Hong Kong. Abby would make sure I didn't get lost en-route and we would be good company for each other throughout the whole experience.

Mary Fox, however, had been busy beavering away and she had arranged for Liz Copper to contact me. I thought Liz was a radio reporter, but she turned out to be an interviewer for BBC Midlands Today. I was terrified of doing a television interview, and Liz and I managed to 'miss' one another for a while, but she finally pinned me down on the Friday as I was about to fly out on the Monday. I know I was reluctant and stressed because time was against me but Liz said, "We can do it Sunday."

"I'm at church Sunday morning at 10.30," I protested.

"We can do it at 9.30," she persisted. I mentioned about the police interest and Darren Teale but she said, "We'll pre-record, let's go ahead, we can catch up with them later." So we did it, the first of many interviews that lay ahead of me in the coming year, and I coped with it, thanks to Liz's sensitivity. I have to say at this point that throughout all the media interest I received nothing but kindness and respect from radio, journalists and television interviewers alike.

Abby and I left the next morning and I was totally unaware of the impact the interview would have when it was broadcast on the following Thursday. Mary emailed me to tell me that the reaction had been extremely positive and emotional and that Mick Harrison, the Police Superintendent, had been superb with his support and had given the television people a live interview that followed on from mine. They also broadcast the fact that drugs had been seized in the Black Country worth 100 million pounds and that men had been arrested. I felt I was in the wrong place at the wrong time but Steffi said to me when she rang, "No Mum, you are just where God wants you to be."

The news continued to reach me on the other side of the world. Darren was inundated with requests for the DVD and I was thrilled that the West Yorkshire Police wanted a copy. The tabloid press and a couple of magazines also wanted me to get in touch but I was a bit nervous of all the publicity, although I did agree to a three way phone interview with Victoria Tennant of Channel 5 Live and Darren in Stoke. Because of the time difference, I did the interview whilst my family were all tucked up in bed. I don't think I slept too well afterwards.

Chapter 8

We got back home in time to celebrate Christmas 2007 as a family, our second without Ben and Mike. Special occasions are never easy now, but we always do them together as best we can.

In the New Year I felt energised and even more determined to get Ben's anti-drugs message out there. I was fired up by the Home Office's announcement at the end of February of a new ten-year drugs strategy that would encourage schools to improve anti-drugs lessons. I decided to write to my local MP but not being a political animal I wrote to the wrong one, Charlotte Atkins. She replied explaining there were strict Parliamentary rules about dealing with other MP's constituents and Alton didn't come into her constituency until the next General Election. However, she kindly agreed to help me and I couldn't have chosen a better MP if I'd tried, as Charlotte was in the process of fighting the closure of the drug advice centre in Leek which had only opened two years previously and had been doing great work.

Charlotte made sure that my email to Jacqui Smith, the then Home Secretary, was delivered, and followed this up with an email telling me that she had met recently with young people both from Staffordshire and from the rest of the country about drugs education and information, and it was through her that I got in contact with our local UK Youth Parliament representative, Joe, who was confident there was a place for Ben's film in education.

I heard personally from Jacqui Smith on the 4th March 2008, saying that she was committed to preventing further young people falling into drug abuse and other families suffering the same experience we had. *"We are committed to drugs education in schools and are currently awaiting the results of an extensive review of drugs education,"* she said, and asked me to forward her a copy of the DVD.

Two days later, Joe contacted Charlotte Atkins regarding the talk she had given to the Youth Parliament and which, because of exams, he had been unable to attend. He said that other young people who were at the event had told him how interested they were in a DVD that Charlotte had talked about regarding a young man in the Staffordshire Moorlands who had tragically died through drug abuse. He said that he was very interested in rolling this out across the Staffordshire Youth Service and other youth agencies such as Connexions. I, of course, sent Joe, who was 15 years old at the time, a copy of 'Sick and Tired'.

I started to feel as though we were getting somewhere, but then came a letter from Vernon Coaker, the then Parliamentary Under Secretary of State, in which he agreed with me that the best way forward is to prevent young people using drugs in the first place, that drug prevention has always been a Government priority and that they had a renewed focus on young people and families in the new Drug Strategy. However, he further went on to say that it is teachers that have the responsibility for the overall drug education programme in their schools as they are best placed to make sure it is relevant and sensitive to local needs. They also decide on the resources used to support this. He suggested that I contact my local authority rather than making contact with individual schools. I also had similar letters from the

Parliamentary Undersecretary of State for Children, Young People and Families.

I reciprocated by replying to Mr Coaker saying I assumed his letter was in response to my sending Ben's DVD to the Home Secretary. Before they closed their file on Ben, however, there were one or two points I wished to get across. The first being that to my knowledge Ben is the only addict who has ever filmed himself, leaving behind over 30 hours of footage, and that the editing was instigated by the probation services who saw the potential. I acknowledged that the DVD was too long for young people at 45 minutes, but that Junction 15, the media company brought in by probation to help Ben with the editing, were more than willing to make this more user-friendly for children and students. There would be no cost to the Government, and neither Junction 15 nor myself were in this for monetary gain – we just wanted to get the message out to this generation that taking drugs is not an option. I wrote that personally I do not believe that young people take the type of drug awareness advertising that is out there at the moment seriously, whereas Ben's story would never leave them and it would certainly get them talking. Mr Coaker had mentioned www.talktofrank, which I said was a very 'colourful' site but surely only accessed when it is too late and the young person already has the problem. I accepted that it was up to me if I wanted to get the DVD out there, but I would have liked the government to endorse it in some way – approve it, if you like. I believed we owed it to young people to give them the truth. It was obvious that what had been used to educate them thus far had not worked.

I then received an apology from the Home Office for the confusion that had been caused. Jacqui Smith had not instigated Vernon Coaker's letter but was still considering the DVD and would respond shortly.

As a result of this, I was then invited to meet with Vernon Coaker at the Home Office and an appointment was set up for the 28th April for 10.00am. I received no rail pass or reimbursement, so I had to phone them and arrange a later train as the earliest affordable train didn't get to Euston until 11.09am. I have to say though that they were very obliging and Mr Coaker rearranged his schedule to accommodate me for 12.30pm.

I didn't want to face officialdom on my own, so they had agreed to Darren coming with me and, believe it or not, the first person that we encountered as we left the tube station near to Marsham Street where the Home Office is situated was a drug addict. He approached us begging for money and there was dried blood encrusted on the side of his face and on his ear where someone had ripped his earring out. It was bizarre, given that we were on our way to a meeting at the highest level to discuss the problem.

Whilst we were waiting for the meeting to start we were offered a cup of tea, and I was horrified that there, in the Home Office, we were offered tea in foreign cups and saucers. Darren and I had travelled from the potteries where the industry was in decline and our own government was flaunting foreign ware. I later pointed this out and was told they used British ware in Westminster!

As well as meeting with Vernon Coaker there were four other people present, all with impressive titles; the Head of Communication Crime Reduction and Community Safety Group, a woman who headed the Cross Cutting Strategy in the Drugs Unit, a woman from FRANK, and Mr Coaker's PA. The meeting lasted an hour and a quarter. A lot was discussed but nothing resolved. I was angry that Vernon Coaker had not watched the DVD prior to our meeting, nor had he been given a copy of correspondence that I had had with Joe, the Youth Parliament representative. He had, however, accessed clips on the Radio Stoke website. The woman from FRANK was anxious to point out that drugs advice was readily available on the website and that they had videos on the site showing drugs abuse. I replied that I had looked at the website and at that time it took some time to load. I thought it was colourful but used animation and actors to get the message across, not real stories. I also said that if young people were accessing the website, surely it meant they had the problem already.

Figures were bandied about and the woman from FRANK said that cannabis use was going down. I asked how they knew this for a fact. Young people don't report to anyone that they've been smoking cannabis this past year but have now stopped. How do they arrive at these figures? Interestingly Peter Hitchens in the Mail of Sunday in November 2011 wrote this short piece on Frank:

> "Feeble Frank is going to pot.
> Parents and teachers who want to stop children taking illegal drugs get little help from the Government. The feeble website 'Talk to Frank' (which we pay for through our taxes) more or less assumes that drug-taking is normal, with lots of matey, slang-infested chat."

My sentiments exactly!

Vernon Coaker had been a teacher in another life, so I was hopeful that I would get the message across that drugs awareness has to start at school, possibly from 12 years onwards, but I rather think that all I got was platitudes, and certainly nothing positive came out of the meeting. At the end of the day I had to accept that it is not the Government's remit to tell schools what to put into their PSHE programmes.

The email from Joe that Vernon Coaker had not read said that Joe had attended a conference at our local council on the issue of substance misuse entitled 'Calling time on substance misuse in Staffordshire'. He had spoken to youth workers, teachers and young people about the issue, and the response from all areas was that the DVD of Ben could be part of a Drugs Education Programme in schools and youth centres.

I met Joe personally in April when we did a radio interview at Radio Stoke. I was very impressed at how well Joe addressed all the questions put to him by the radio presenter, Stuart George. I felt that Joe was an answer to my prayers; he was young, articulate, enthusiastic and committed to getting Ben's message out to schoolchildren. He had watched the DVD with some friends and they had all found the DVD to be incredibly moving and believed that it could make serious changes in the attitudes of young people who were curious about drugs or who had already started dabbling. It was hard to remember that he was just 15 years old.

Joe was very quickly on the ball and met with the Staffordshire Advisory Body where Members of the Youth Parliament give their advice on Staffordshire County Council policy. At this meeting, Joe talked about the DVD and received positive feedback from them. The chairman would arrange for Joe to attend a meeting of the full council to present the DVD to them and Joe would also approach the Youth Parliament to see if they would provide some funding.

May 19th – May 23rd 2008 was National Tackling Drugs Week, and I was absolutely thrilled with the work that was being done by Joe. He had written to assure me that DAT (Staffordshire Drug and Alcohol Team) were now involved. I felt that if DAT were on board then the battle was half won. DAT are a government agency, and apparently every local authority has one of these teams, and Vernon Coaker had promised that they would be contacted. I was also very excited that the Youth Parliament was interested in the distribution of the DVD. If they could see the potential of the DVD as a resource for warning young people off drugs and educating them as to the dangers, then their opinion has surely got to be paramount and those adults involved in implementing the distribution of the DVD must surely take them seriously. How wrong was I!

By the middle of 2008 the DVD had been seen by many across the country – police authorities, prisons, agencies, college courses, families etc. and we had received nothing but positive feedback and encouragement. So for me, education was the last frontier, if you like.

I was able to update Vernon Coaker on the 13th August. Although I had heard nothing further from the Home Office, I thanked him if there had been any input into the agencies concerned. I was able to tell him that Joe, the Youth Parliament representative for Staffordshire Moorlands, had done an amazing amount of work and had a strong commitment to the necessity for this DVD to get into education. I wrote that Joe had secured funding to run a two day residential in half term when eight young people from across the country would meet with Drugs and Youth Workers to edit the DVD, with Junction 15's support, to make the format, length and content suitable for young people. This had the backing of our County DAT team, Staffordshire County Council and Staffordshire Youth Council, not forgetting the Youth Parliament and Staffordshire's Youth Action Council who had provided the funding for the residential weekend. It was hoped that the finished project would be piloted across Staffordshire in 2009.

Chapter 9

There had been a tremendous amount of publicity locally, both through Radio Stoke and our local newspapers, and this precipitated a phone call from a freelance journalist, Eugene Henderson. Eugene had been following the publicity about Ben's footage and felt that he could get an article into the Sunday Express if I would be willing. He thought that Ben's story had a very wide appeal and he was extremely persuasive, thank goodness, as I had been wary of the press in the 12 months since Ben died and wasn't happy with an article that a local paper had written. He interviewed me over the phone and promised to let me know what transpired.

Two or three weeks went by and I heard nothing, and, never the patient type, I phoned him up. Eugene told me that he hadn't been able to get the Express' interest but that he knew someone at the Daily Mail and asked if I had any objection to him having a go there. Success! I was interviewed over the phone from a reporter from the Mail by the name of Jaye Narain, and when it was published on Friday, 30th May I was delighted with the result. Don't forget that I had avoided press interviews wherever possible. In my scrabbled head was the thought, "This is about Ben, it's not about me." I know, it's obvious to me now, Ben wasn't around to promote the message he wanted to get over, there was only me. The one page spread in the Daily Mail said "An Addict's Last Days" and quoted me accurately that Ben had left over 30 hours of film footage that would be turned into an educational resource.

The following day, again in the Daily Mail, the well-known writer and journalist Ray Connolly wrote a two page spread with the dramatic headline "Murdered by Glamour" and stating that Britain is in the grip of a lethal hypocrisy. "Whilst we revere rock stars, models and comedians who glamorise drug addiction, people like Ben will continue to die." There were photos of Ben at different stages of his life, alongside a photo of Amy Winehouse, who has tragically also lost her life since.

Joe in the meantime was beavering away with the education pack. He had had a meeting with DAT and they would not only support it but would look at funding some of the production costs. He also had had confirmation from the Head of the Staffordshire Youth Service that full backing from their staff would be given. Over the summer Joe, together with staff from the Youth Services and DAT, would be researching existing programmes to make Ben's the best resource out there. In October, half-term week, the plan was to form and take a team of 8 young people away for a residential weekend to work on the DVD and pack with the support of different agencies. The promise was that the pack would be in schools in Staffordshire in 2009.

I was being interviewed by Radio Stoke on the morning the Daily Mail article came out and was hit by the interest the minute I switched on my mobile phone. ITV News had been trying to reach me, and Darren was leaving me frantic messages. I was supposed to be going to visit my friend, Iris, after the Radio Stoke interview, but I had to ring her to let her know what was going on. "The ITN news people are coming to the house to interview me, Iris," I said. My nervousness must have showed, because Iris said, "I'm coming over, don't worry, you'll be great."

When I got back to my cottage in my quiet little village, where I have probably devalued all the properties, it seemed as though mayhem had descended. My cottage has little or no drive and crammed onto it was an ITN Central News van sporting a very large aerial dish– I now understand that the news item is edited there and then inside the vehicle and then magically transported to the TV studio. My home was suddenly filled with cameras, crew and an interviewer by the name of Tim Rogers, obviously not a relation! As things were kicking off, Iris arrived, together with another vehicle carrying the crew of ITN National News, but they had to wait outside until the first interview was done and dusted.

It all got a bit bizarre. Somewhere in between these two interviews I had two phone calls, and the first was from the BBC. Could I get down to London to be interviewed on BBC Breakfast News early Saturday morning, they asked. I agreed, and after putting the phone down one of the ITN crew said, "You're not going on your own, surely."

Iris said, "I can come with you."

"Ring them up and tell them you want two rail tickets and a hotel booking for two," the ITN girl urged.

"Oh I don't like to fuss, I couldn't possibly ask them."

"I will," Iris butted in, and that's what she did and they agreed! Brilliant, because quite honestly I don't think I could have managed on my own.

The ITN national news people were still with me when the phone rang again. "Hello, this is the Lorraine Kelly show, we would really love you to be on the show on Monday." I, of course, agreed, but this time did not hesitate to ask for two rail tickets and a hotel booking for two. This was no problem, but then ten minutes later this call was followed by a call from the Breakfast Show people with Fern and Philip also requesting an interview for the Monday morning. I told them I had already agreed to the Lorraine Show interview and the girl on the other end of the phone was very put out. "Cancel them" she said.

"I can't do that, I've promised them already, and anyway aren't you all ITV?" Wrong thing to say...It was a frantic weekend. Only hours after the double page spread in the Daily Mail I had been interviewed at home by local and national ITN news people, and I was on my way that evening to a breakfast interview with the BBC, thankfully with Iris by my side. That very same day Darren had also been inundated with phone calls and emails. He had been approached by no less than three independent film makers interested in taking Ben's story further. He had immediately turned down two of them, one of which had offered him £25,000 to hand over the tapes. Don't forget that Darren had the copyright, and could have done so quite legitimately. It is the measure of the man that he refused because he would have had no control over how they would be used, and Darren's motives for the footage were as honourable as mine. He was, however, interested in one of the companies, and he asked me if he could look into it further, so in the same week I was going to London Darren was doing the same.

We got to London late on the Friday night and, as we were about to turn in, the phone rang. It was the BBC, saying that I was there to do an interview on Breakfast TV with Susanna and Ben at 9.30, but would I mind also doing an earlier one at 7.00am? No pressure there then, and not much sleep either. A car collected us in good time and we were taken to the Green Room, where I waited along with other interviewees. The Green Room at the BBC is very small and accommodates only a few before it is overcrowded and spilling out into the corridor. People like to talk and they are keen to share why they are there. One was to discuss public smoking, another was the son of a famous BBC journalist talking about his restaurant, someone on some ecological issue and then my turn. That rather killed the conversation!

As a license payer, you will be glad to know that the BBC doesn't throw your money around recklessly. There was no meal provided for us at the hotel when we arrived late on the Friday evening, and makeup consisted of a lady who came into the green room with a bum bag from which she flourished a brush and a box of powder. She then proceeded to run this across the bridge of my nose and that was it! Maybe she felt she couldn't gild the lily, but the biggest surprise was the studio, which was a large space with Susanna and Ben on a raised platform in the middle of the room and, apart from me, only one other person present. This man took me to my seat next to the interview table and proceeded to wire me up with a microphone. He then departed to a computer in the corner of the studio where he alone operated the bank of cameras situated in front of the interview area. It was a vast contrast to the This Morning studios, where the place was literally buzzing with bodies and where the many cameras were operated individually by real people.

Susanna and Ben were very kind and sympathetic, as everyone in the media has been throughout all of this. One interviewer said, "I had pre-conceived ideas of drug addicts but Ben's story has changed all that, I now see addicts differently." I cannot fault them, I have received nothing but sympathy and respect and I thank them for that.

A car took us back to Euston station for our journey back home but, of course, we had to return the next day for the Lorraine Kelly interview on the Monday morning. This was a much more entertaining experience – not the interview, that was nerve-racking, but the rest of it was entertaining. Again, we were met at Euston station and taken to a hotel, but this time an evening meal was provided. After an all you can eat breakfast, a car arrived and we were taken to the studios.

No quick brush across the nose with the commercial station. They have a very well stocked make up studio where my whole persona was dealt with – eyes, face, lips, hair – I didn't want to wash it off at bedtime, I felt so glamorous. The place was heaving with well-known faces from the television, and in the makeup chair next to me was Marlon from Emmerdale, a programme Ben had always followed. Emmerdale did a wonderful storyline recently about a young girl who got into drugs, which was very realistic and ran for several weeks. It satisfies me greatly that at last heroin and other addictions are out in the public domain and people are more open about the problem.

Lorraine was very professional, but having said that I was straight in, onto the chair, face to face with her, with no prior meeting to put me more at my ease. It's funny the reaction you get from friends after an appearance on television. I thought that if they said anything at all it would be something like, "You really got your point across," or, "It must have been an ordeal for you but you managed really well," but no. One friend admired my necklace, another said, "I never knew your cottage was so lovely," and a third, Mary Fox actually, asked me where I got my green cardigan from! Bizarre.

As in the news items that had gone out previously, both on television and radio, I stressed that my greatest aim was to get the footage into education and that I had Joe and the Youth Parliament on my side in this. It was certainly a manic weekend but there was no mistake, Ben's story was out there.

Chapter 10

As I said previously, Darren was negotiating with a company called Gecko Productions, an independent television production company under the auspices of their Chief Executive, Vivien McGrath. When Darren told me who he was dealing with, I researched her work record on the internet and was very impressed. A lot of her TV documentaries were stories of real people who had undergone traumatic experiences in their lives, including the documentary for Channel 4 'The Girls Who Were Found Alive' about two young girls who were abducted and rescued five days later, and 'The Girl in the Box', made for Channel 5 about a 17 year old hitchhiker who was kidnapped and kept in a box for 7 years. When Viv rang me to discuss the making of the documentary, she made it very clear that my views and wishes were paramount. Vivien promised that I would be kept informed every step of the way and that is what she did.

Once Darren and I agreed to her making the documentary, she very early on in the proceedings said she felt that Sky TV would be interested. I had the same reaction as I had when the daily tabloids were after me for an interview - dismay! I didn't have Sky myself at that time and I thought that they weren't in the serious business of documentary making. In actual fact, I wasn't too far from the truth, but when the documentary was aired just a few months later the newspapers applauded Sky for moving into more serious documentary making. In fact, it drew higher audience viewing figures than Sky had ever received before for a documentary.

Vivien tells me that after her meeting with Darren, who would co-produce the documentary, she had to decide on whom to ask to direct it. Apparently one name came into her mind - Olly Lambert. Olly is a young award winning cinematographer, again with a string of credible, mainly war-based, documentaries behind him. She arranged a meeting with Olly, who at first wasn't interested. He felt the subject was too dark and that the material was shocking. "I'd never seen anything like it, I was literally speechless," he said. "I had never seen any material before that had shown someone so close to a personal abyss." Olly's reaction was not one of immediate acceptance, and he needed to go away and think about it. The next morning he decided that, because of the impact it had had on him, he would do it.

Darren and I had talked some twelve months previous about doing a fresh documentary using some of Ben's footage, but incorporating interviews with the family. That hadn't materialised, mainly due to cost I think. Darren had done everything to do with 'Sick and Tired' for nothing. He had to constantly mail copies of the DVD right from the early days, as Ben had received a lot of publicity locally thanks to Radio Stoke. He was doing all this for free because like me he believed that Ben had an important and unique message to tell, but I was aware that he had a business to run and a living to make, so the documentary Darren wanted to do had to go on the backburner.

Olly and Darren came to see me in early August 2008. Olly said that driving into the village was a shock. He would have thought that Alton was the last frontier, if you like, where drugs were concerned. The last place you would have thought that there would be the problem with its beautiful houses and attractive little pubs. Was nowhere safe anymore?

I had my daughter, Steffi, come over for the meeting as I was a bit nervous, but I needn't have been. Olly breezed in saying something like, "Hi Anne, I feel I know you so well from Ben's film." Fortunately this didn't faze me, but he used the same line with Emma when he went to talk to her, incidentally a day earlier than he had arranged, and it freaked her out. He said he would be directing the film, and Darren and Viv would be co-producing it. He went to great lengths to reassure me that his intentions for the documentary were on a par with ours, and that the kind of film he wanted to make would be respectful, to us as a family but also to the memory of Ben. If the documentary could serve as some kind of warning to others about the road that drugs can lead you down, then he thought that they would have served Ben's hard work well. What a charmer, I thought, and I was impressed and completely won over.

I understand that Darren and Olly met with Andrew O'Connell from Sky television, who were now on board. Olly asked Andrew what was the brief – what did he want from the documentary? Andrew said, "Just go away and make the best documentary that you can," and Andrew kept very much to his word, taking out only four minutes of the finished article to keep it within the time frame. How amazing was that!

I furnished Olly and Darren with a list of friends of Ben's who might be able to contribute something, and I know that the two of them set about interviewing. Time was of the essence because from beginning to end they had only been given six weeks to complete. The most important name on the list was Emma, and she did agree to meet with Olly, but I think she was very anxious at that time to keep her relationship with Ben secret. She had an exceptionally good job and just didn't want people to know her involvement with a heroin addict, and who could blame her for that. Eventually Emma asked that their relationship be kept out of the documentary and we had to respect her wishes. Only a couple of Ben's friends preferred not to talk to Olly and Darren; most were happy to help and I am grateful to them for their contribution.

I had to dig around in my memory for things that might be of interest for the documentary, and I was reminded that during those last two years he decided to go to France to do cold turkey, using Mike's car for the journey. Needless to say he got himself arrested by the French police, kept in the cells overnight and was up in court the next day. He was ordered out of the country and told not to come back. He reckons he had a severe body beating from the police and that the cold turkey didn't work. We did try to dissuade him before he left, saying that he could do the same job in the highlands of Scotland, but no, Ben wanted to do it in France. Ben loved France and we'd had many family holidays there over the years, but he'd never have been able to travel there again.

Things were moving swiftly, and Olly expressed that the job was becoming more than just a job for him. He had been simply stunned by some of the footage and was committed to the project as there was no doubt in his mind that it could and should become an important document about the risks and dangers of drugs and addiction. He felt it was his responsibility to humanise the story, to force people to engage with it, as he was sure that it had the potential to change and even save lives. Olly said that, "Ben was a man who loved and was loved, and was not just an addict, and that if the film had any purpose whatsoever it would be to show and warn both adults and children that even the 'ordinary' people from 'nice' homes with close family and friends could still be brought down by drugs and their addiction to them. It felt like a story of our time."

Olly and Darren had only about three weeks to complete the documentary rough cut, so it was quite a manic period with Olly coming and going. As well as interviewing us and Ben's friends, he had to go through all of Ben's footage to decide what he could use and what he couldn't. He told me later that it was very clear that Ben wanted his story made into a documentary and that Ben even looked at the camera in one shot and said what he wanted leaving in. "It was as if he was directing me," said Olly. Once all the interviewing was complete, Olly left for Spain for three weeks, where he and Dan Glendenning, his editor, worked on the finished article. He was working to a very tight deadline as the film had been accepted for premiering at the prestigious Sheffield Documentary Film Festival in November 2008 and Olly wanted to bring the finished article to show the family whilst he was en-route to Sheffield.

Quite a crowd gathered in my house for that showing. As well as my immediate family, I wanted Mary Fox to be there, along with my good friends Iris and Dorothy. I know that Olly was very nervous about our reaction but he needn't have been. I would tell Olly that, "As Ben's mother, it became so much easier to hate Ben those last few years than to love him, but Olly, you have helped restore the balance. I really want to thank you for that and you too, Darren. I know, Darren, that it must have been hard for you to let the footage go into another's hands to realise the vision that you had all along for Ben."

Watching the film was so hard, I felt as though my heart was being wrenched from my body. I had to watch things that no mother should have to know about their child, and as it drew to a close I fled from the lounge howling. Olly called after me, "No Anne, stay, I want you to see this." What he wanted me to see was the fact that he had given Ben the credit for the film as if Ben had still been alive. How generous was that. Olly has a truly rare gift – he is a real human being. I had put my trust in him and in Darren, and I wasn't let down.

Chapter 11

I had been invited to the Sheffield Film Festival along with Sarah and Phil. Darren and Andrew from Junction 15 would travel separately. My youngest twin grandchildren, Megan and Josh, who were in their first year at Sheffield University, would also join us. It would be quite a night out. There were many films to be shown that night and the place was really buzzing with filmmakers and public alike. We were to meet up in the public bar prior to the showing, and Olly very soon came and found us and tried to put me at my ease. I was very anxious. How would it be received? Would it be too shocking? My stomach was churning, and suddenly the crowd hushed and people fell away in front of me, forming a channel. Andrew O'Connell had entered the room and it was as if Moses was parting the Dead Sea. He did say a few words to me along the lines of, "Thank you again for letting us make this documentary," but little else, and then he was gone again. I learned later that he was not in a good mood. The film was being shown in one of the smallest rooms. People were queuing to get in to see it and many, including delegates, were turned away. I think he was trying to get the showing moved, but there was nothing else available and it was almost time for curtain up.

This was only the second time I had seen the documentary, which had been given the title 'Ben: Diary of a Heroin Addict', and for my grandchildren it was the first and possibly even the last time they had seen it. I was on the second row behind

Andrew O'Connell, with Megan and Josh directly behind me on the third row, much too close to the action I think. Olly and Darren were much further back and I couldn't see them at all. The film ran without a hitch, and you could have heard a pin drop – no coughing, no shuffling, nothing that is except a strangled sob from my grandson. You have to remember that not only were we watching Ben's self destruction but the kids had to see their beloved Grandad, who for them was always full of fun and life, looking sad and defeated and gone from them forever.

The film that was shown was the full version with the four minutes that was edited out for television, so all in all it ran for about 45 minutes and then the lights went up to....deadly silence! I didn't dare turn in my seat because I honestly thought everyone behind me must have quietly got up and gone. The silence lasted for about a minute and then applause broke out. Relief. Olly came forward and we did a question and answer session.

Everyone connected with the documentary was on a high. It had been a success. Lots of people wanted to talk to us and some were visibly upset. After about an hour, though, I couldn't cope any longer. Everyone was crowding in on me and I wanted to go home. When Ben and then Mike died I accepted every invitation offered, even though I would end up hiding myself away somewhere. I remember going to a Marks and Spencer's open night with some friends ending up crouched behind a clothing rail to hide as I kept bumping into people I knew. At parties I would sometimes escape for up to 20 minutes locked in someone's loo. So for me 'escaping' was a familiar reaction and, true to form, thanks to Phil and Sarah, I made my way home.

There was a lot of feedback from that evening. Viv said it had been the talk of the Festival. Apparently there had never been a queue as long as that for standby tickets, and Olly had been inundated with requests for copies of the DVD. The Documentary Filmmakers Group had asked for a screening in advance of transmission and the channel controller of Sky had asked that it be pushed as an awards contender. Olly had already been approached at the Festival by one awards company, which was unheard of in Olly's experience. In December, Viv sent me the results of the survey that the 1565 delegates were asked to fill it in to find out what they thought of the different elements of the Festival. 362 people completed the survey representing a good sample of 23%. I was given the results of Ben's documentary. 90% rated the film as 'Good' or above, with 28% rating it as 'Very Good' and 41% as 'Excellent', which made 'Ben: Diary of a Heroin Addict' one of the most highly rated films of the 2008 documentary festival.

I wrote to Olly affirming that he and Darren had more than fulfilled my expectations for the film. Right at the beginning of all that had happened, my aim had been to get across to people that drug addicts, heroin in particular, are worthy of consideration. I wanted to show that there is more to them than the problem, and Olly and Darren had certainly succeeded in doing this.

The film was screened on the 8th December 2008, and the publicity before and after was overwhelming. Most importantly, it was positive and non-judgemental. Every TV magazine had it as their 'choice' for documentary viewing. The Times covered it on Saturday, Sunday and Monday, and then Andrew Billen in their review wrote:

"There were no soaring seagulls in this film, mainly because the bulk of it was filmed by Ben himself. He had been a runner in a production company and while his camerawork started shakily it grew in confidence. He videoed himself injecting into his groin, driving while high and slumping under the table during a meal. He knew he was dying. His last wish was that his video tapes be cut into a documentary. He could not have asked for more than last night's."

Someone from Channel 5 contacted Viv to say:
"I watched your superb documentary about Ben last night – it was incredibly honest and very moving. I take a particular interest in this subject as I lost two close friends to heroin as a student and I actually work on the Talk to Frank helpline. This is the most accurate portrayal of heroin addiction I have ever seen. A brave film and a brave commission."

It was covered in The Wright Stuff on Channel 5, and Matthew Wright said that it should be shown in every school in the land. My sentiments exactly.

Yes, the publicity was amazing, but it was the behind the scenes things that really thrilled me. A homeless hostel had been in touch with Sky, as they wanted a copy of the documentary to use to train staff, and Sky had sent a copy of the DVD out to Jacqui Smith and several other MPs. Sky assigned a member of their staff as my contact, Colin Watkins, and I would like to thank him here publicly for all his kindness throughout this difficult period.

To date, the documentary has been shown 27 times on national television and has been distributed globally and seen across Europe, Australia and Canada, to my knowledge. It was shortlisted in 2009 for a BAFTA award, and nominated in the last three for a FOCAL International Award. Focal is the world's leading award for documentaries using archive footage. Ben's DVD was nominated in the training or education production category. In the same year, 2009, it was also nominated down to the final three in the French FTV International documentary film festival. A young man in America put it on YouTube, and, despite it having been removed three times due to distribution rights, it has had way over 1,500,000 hits and still averages 2,000 every two or three days.

Chapter 12

In early 2010, Darren told me that he had been contacted by The Burnet Institute in Melbourne, Australia. The Burnet Institute is a leading Australian medical research and public health organisation focused on improving the health of disadvantaged and marginalized groups. They work at international and regional level, with governments, civil society and communities in more than 15 countries working to reduce the impact and spread of HIV, promoting sexual and reproductive health and improving the health of children, youths and older people. Since 2004 the Institute has been responsible for the organisation of a film festival that takes place over three days within the International Drugs and Harm Reduction Conference, which has been held in many countries across the world for the past 21 years. 2010 was their 21st anniversary, and the conference was to be held in Liverpool, where it was first launched all those years ago at the BT Convention Centre. Ben's film had been shown three times on Australian television, and the Burnet Institute wanted to enter it into the film festival. Darren and I were invited to attend.

The conference and film festival are not open to the general public, only to delegates who come from over 80 countries, and I understand that more than 1400 attended. Rebecca Winter from the Burnet Institute informed me that there had been 75 films entered for the festival from which 35 would be shown over the three day period, and that these had been submitted by 21 countries. Of course, Darren and I accepted the invitation to attend in April 2010, but then on March 30th we were informed that a panel had judged the films prior to the festival and that 'Ben: Diary of a Heroin Addict' had been awarded the 'Best Film' award. We were delighted that the film had been given this honour and agreed not only to keep it 'under our hats' until the conference but also to stay over to the following day for the presentation.

It was an exhilarating experience for us both and it certainly brought home to me that drugs are a worldwide horror story. We had the opportunity to watch a few of the other films that had been entered and one of them to me stood out as outstanding and I was amazed that the Australian people hadn't chosen it. It was called 'Bastardy' and was about an elderly Aborigine actor called Jack Charles, who had managed to maintain a career as a notable actor but was also a burglar and a heroin addict. He lived on the streets and everyone knew him. In the film it showed him reunited with his brother, who had been taken from the family as a child and made to live and work on a farm where he had been so mistreated and beaten that it had damaged his brain. I wept throughout the film as it was such a touching story.

As well as showing Ben's documentary at the festival, it was also given a public showing at the FACT cinema, and I was asked to do a question and answer session after both screenings. I met and talked to people from China, America, Malaysia and the United Arab Emirates, who were hosting the festival in 2011, and they all expressed an interest in showing the film in their countries. They all confirmed to me that Ben's film was unique because Ben himself had 'told the story'.

When the award was presented to Darren and to myself, representing Ben, by Gary Reid from the World Health Organisation South East Asian Office based in New Delhi, for the first time in many years I allowed myself to feel proud of Ben, that in the midst of all the misery he put himself through he was able to articulate his story in the hope that it would not only deter others, especially young people, but also educate what it's like to be an addict.

Of course, I don't know everything that has happened around Ben's documentary, and I probably never will, but I do know that almost daily something arrives in my e mail or message boxes through Facebook or YouTube. I can also pick up on some things through the internet and again in March 2010 I discovered that the film was having a Vancouver Premiere at the Pacific Cinematheque. There was to be a post-screening discussion with a psychiatrist working in the fields of addiction and chronic severe mental illness at Vancouver General Hospital, an addiction psychiatrist with Richmond Mental Health Services and a Clinical Instructor with the UBC Department of Psychiatry. The moderator was the Clinical Professor in the Department of Psychiatry at the University of British Columbia. The conclusion drawn was:

> "Either way, for most outside of the Mental Health system, it does point out that addictions can happen to anyone and in any socio-economic class. The common link is that the collateral damage affects everyone in the social circle, thus anyone can be an unintended victim to this horrible circumstance." In June 2010, I was contacted by a solicitor who had practised in England but had moved to Townsville, Australia. She asked for

a copy of Ben's DVD to be used within the confines of the court.

Things started to quieten down, but I had other things to occupy me. Our local probation service wanted me to speak at their annual staff conference and I was happy to oblige. I had done one other public talk, and the venue for that had been Port Vale Football Club. Probation's venue was Stoke City Football Club. I had gone up in the league! Mike and Ben would have been so excited, as they had been avid Stoke City supporters, often on a Saturday going out to watch their team only to come home miserable because of a poor result. How thrilled they would be now to see Stoke in the Premier League. I was happy to do the talk for probation. After all, Ben said, "Probation was the best thing that had happened to me in a long time." I had hoped that Ben's probation officer, Neil, who had done so much for Ben, would be there, but unfortunately he wasn't able to attend. I have, however, met with Neil several times since then and he knows how grateful I am.

I have had the opportunity to talk to young offenders about Ben's story and I find this a real privilege. By and large, these young kids are respectful and courteous, and they ask questions that are relevant to what I have been talking to them about. Occasionally one of them will empathise with me and say, "Don't know how you do it, it must be real hard." The feedback I get from these sessions is encouraging, and one young lad, whose mum was a heroin addict who hung herself, has really turned his life round. Someone said to me once, "If it only stops one young person from going down the same route as your son it will all be worth it," and so it is. I'm happy with that result.

Chapter 13

"There should be a strong focus on evidence-based education so current drug users and those who may consider taking drugs are fully aware of the risks."
    Lord Adebowale, Chief Executive of the drugs charity Turning Point

I know this and you know this, so why can't those who are paid to implement drugs education know it?

We all had such high hopes in those early dealings with Staffordshire County Council. In mid-2008 Joe was still at school, but was totally committed and confident that Ben's story would be developed into a teaching aid that could be used, not just in Staffordshire but across the country. He had DAT's full support and they would hopefully not only provide some of the funding but would also help with the written part of the pack. Joe also had the backing of Staffordshire Youth Services.

In the summer, with his GCSEs under his belt, Joe left school and made the momentous decision not to go into sixth form but to continue his education on the job and defer university until a later date. He was then offered a job as a paid Participation Support Worker for Staffordshire's newly appointed Children's Commissioner, and accepted it. Staffordshire was fortunate to have this facility, as the Commissioner's role was to ensure that young people's views are taken into account when planning and providing services for children in the county. She was 100% behind what Joe was trying to achieve, but unfortunately the post didn't last long, not in our county anyway. At the time, it all seemed like an answer to my prayers. With Joe in situ we had to succeed, how could we fail? Joe has always said that he wasn't paid to work on Ben's DVD and that everything he did had to be done extra to his other duties. Having said that, though, the Council were happy to pay the salary of Donna, the youth worker who was seconded to help Joe one day a week on the education pack.

Donna and Joe's first step was to find a team of young people who would be instrumental in putting together the education pack, and in August of that year Youth Services across the county recruited a handful of young people to work on the packs. I was invited to the evening meeting when they first met to get to know one another, and I was very impressed with Joe's leadership qualities and the fact that a council worker had been seconded to assist Joe with the drugs education project. Donna was from the Youth Services and had successfully worked on drugs and alcohol projects in the past. She also had a good rapport with the youngsters present and they were soon playing the sort of games that get you mingling.

These young people who had volunteered amongst others for the task were from all walks of life. Some had dabbled with drugs, one more seriously, some had the problem in the family, one had experienced homelessness, and a couple of them had led exemplary lives, but only one knew anything about Ben's DVD. They were all in their teens. From this group would come the eight who would go forward with the serious business of developing a six lesson pack with named interactive activities and discussions interspersed with relevant clips from Ben's film footage. This would be a resource that PSHE teachers could deliver to their classes with confidence – each lesson would have a balance of games and activities, opportunities for open discussion, and only the right clips from Ben's footage would be used that would reinforce what the lesson was endeavouring to get across to the kids. I never intended from the start that Ben's DVD would be shown in its entirety to school children. It is very harrowing and difficult even for some adults to watch, but Ben left 40 hours of film and Darren was more than willing to help with the editing.

Getting it into education had become my passion. Drug taking in this country is such a big problem, and if it were a measles epidemic everyone would be jumping to eradicate it, and an epidemic it is, with more and more 'designer' drugs coming onto the market. It has to stop before it starts because, believe me, there is no lasting cure once they become hooked'. Granted, some do manage to get clean, but they are never cured. Ben started on drugs here in Alton when he was a teenager through, I believe, ignorance. I am sure that if he had known the full picture he would never have been tempted to try them in the first place. It needs to be got across to children that drugs are not an option, they are a definite no-go, and youngsters must be taught that, at best, drugs will affect them mentally and ruin their looks – at worst it could kill them.

I think the 'team' met several times before the residential weekend at Standon Bowers Outdoor Education Centre in June 2009. £5,000 to fund this had come through YAK, the Youth Action Council. This time, both Darren and I were invited to spend Saturday afternoon with them, and we watched the whole of Ben's 'Sick and Tired' DVD together. I think this may have been the first time that the young people had watched the whole film and, to be honest, it did really upset one of the girls, and we had to pause the showing of it, but after a break she did come back and continued watching it to the end. Accompanying them for the weekend were two workers from DAT, the county's Drugs and Alcohol Action Team, who were still very much on board.

In March 2010, a larger group of young people had a second residential weekend at the Premier Inn in Stafford to develop confidence when they would be given the task of delivering the pack that month to 13 young people who were either on ASBOs or who had low concentration. It was felt that if the pack worked with them the council would have achieved its aims.

I was always in very close communication with Joe, both through the email and on the phone. I think I could paper my house with the emails that passed between us and with Darren. Joe obviously had a mighty task on his hands trying to convince councillors and committee members that Ben's DVD was the best way forward for drugs education in Staffordshire. He also had the problem of a change of council in 2009 with new councillors and new policies to contend with. I think now though with hindsight that I was very trusting in Joe and in the Council. At an early meeting with Joe and Darren, we discussed going down the private funding route and Robbie William's charity, 'Give it Sum', was brought up. Joe persuaded Darren and I that this was something we could fall back on if the Council failed to deliver, but he also warned us that it could take four years or more to get policies through. And almost four years it took them, to bin the pack!

Again, looking back over those years I had no communication or meeting with the council. Everything was done through Joe at venues away from the council offices. At that time Government were stressing that young people had to be listened to and that their views had to be taken seriously. The Youth Parliament had a lot of credibility and, of course, Joe was their local representative. I now think that perhaps the whole thing was officialdom pandering to this concept, being seen listening to and working with young people – in other words doing the 'talk' but ultimately not the 'walk'.

In August 2009, Joe was in touch with me about a survey on drugs education that was to be circulated to all 55 high schools, 14 middle schools and 23 special schools in the county. I was told that Government and education now recognise that children's opinions count and should be taken into consideration in important issues such as drugs, sex, and so on. Joe said they needed a huge response from schoolchildren for it to have any impact and that it was crucial from a funding point of view. He asked me if I would ring a few of them to encourage the schools to get the pupils to fill in the survey. Joe told me I could use the Youth Parliament and the County Council's name to help me get through to either the head teacher or the PSHE teacher. I rang all 92 schools over a two week period and only failed to make contact with three. Can anyone tell me why the head teachers were always in meetings and deputy heads teaching? I am, however, nothing if not tenacious, and I spoke to someone in authority in the remaining 89. It paid off because almost 4000 young people filled in the questionnaire, unheard of in Joe's opinion. He said that similar requests in the past usually resulted in only two or three hundred responding.

Liz Copper from BBC Midlands Today interviewed Joe and I at Joe's home about the survey as Joe was in the process of collating the results on his laptop. The information gleaned from the survey was that one of the most effective tools in their drugs education came from watching DVDs. By far and away the biggest percentage supported the addition of 'real life stories', with half of the respondents voting for ex-users being the best deliverers. Ben's story ticked all their boxes, but then twelve months later the council told me that children didn't want shock tactics! Ben's is a real life story, told by the young person experiencing it. It shows quite clearly the effects that drugs and alcohol will have on a person's wellbeing, lifestyle and looks. It pulls no punches, it tells it as it is, and I think that young people need and deserve the truth – it's not enough anymore to wrap their education up in cartoon type images. Drugs, and I include alcohol as a drug, are not take seriously enough – they are joked about by comedians, glamorised often by the press when taken by celebrities, even accepted as part of our culture. The public perceive heroin addicts as disturbed young people from dysfunctional homes. Ben's film shows that drugs have the same effect on anyone who gets caught up in its usage. I think that possibly the most effective part of Ben's story is that he comes over as a likeable young man, who takes the responsibility of his actions totally on his own shoulders, that he is loved and in return loves his family – but even the love and remorse that he shows can't get in the way of the addiction and he is shown to lie and manipulate to get what he wants.

Chapter 14

Sam and his family were coming home from New Zealand for Christmas of 2009. We were all so excited that the family would be together again, and we had the best of times, although everything that could go wrong did. My central heating broke down and throughout the Christmas period I had to periodically go up to the airing cupboard and 'blow dry' some electrical part using my hair dryer. My washing machine door fell off and the repair couldn't again be done because it was the holiday season. One of my grandsons was violently sick one night with no washing machine to do the necessary cleaning. He and the rest of my New Zealand family went off the following day for a three day trip to Paris and they were all sick whilst there. My grandsons were having a snowball fight outside and one of them put a snowball through the back window of my car - I had to go into Hanley to get the window replaced on Boxing Day! I put my frozen turkey to defrost in my cold oven the night before Christmas Eve leaving the drop down door open an inch and my cat, Olly, managed to force the door down and pull out the oven dish and turkey onto the floor. I found the turkey the next morning on the floor, still in the dish but minus a leg and a good part of the breast. I had to purchase a fresh turkey on Christmas Eve at a horrendous extra cost. The grandson who had been sick first fell in the snow, cutting open his chin, and had to go to hospital to have it attended to, but we had the best Christmas. We were together, a family again. How

Mike would have loved that. Christmas was his favourite time of the year, and he always made it special for all of us. I remember also that when Sam told us he was moving his family to New Zealand, and this was before Ben died, Mike said, "I feel as if I am losing both of my sons."

Whilst Sam and Jayne were here, Joe contacted me and said that the pack mock-up was ready and asked if he, Donna and two of the young people who had helped with the content, could come and present it to the family. That is what they did on the 21st December 2009. It must have been quite daunting for them because my family had four teachers and a sixth former amongst them, and Sam teaches PSHE at his school in New Zealand. They didn't go through all of the six lessons, but chose a couple for us to interact with. One was on identification of the different types of drugs and the other was on stereotyping. Ben's film footage didn't come into this presentation, it was just to show us the format of how the lessons would be presented.

Ofsted reported in July 2010 that:

> "Lack of discrete curriculum time in a quarter of the schools visited, particularly the secondary schools, meant that programmes of study were not covered in full. The areas that suffered included aspects of sex and relationships education, education about drugs, including alcohol, and mental health issues, that were not covered at all or were dealt with superficially." Joe reported that Staffordshire County Council had agreed funding for the design and printing through their Central Print Department of 55 packs to be distributed to Staffordshire schools to be used with young people at Key Stage 4, with the remaining 45 to be sent to the

Youth Services, Connexions and the Youth Offending Services. The School Improvement Division would pay for drug and alcohol delivery training on how to use the pack. The six lesson pack would be piloted in three schools in Staffordshire in September 2010, with an official launch in November to which all Middle, High and Special School heads and their PSHE's would be invited, together with youth services and other interested parties. At that time I was told that 16 other councils across the Midlands had expressed an interest in the finished pack.

My youngest grandchild was in middle school at this time and she was approached by her PSHE teacher and asked to do a presentation about her Uncle Ben to a class assembly. She refused as she felt she couldn't deliver it without getting emotional. About six months later, her PSHE teacher approached her again, and this time she was persuaded. This must have been the hardest thing in the world for her to do but she did it for her Uncle Ben because she said, "Uncle Ben wanted to stop other children from doing drugs, that was why he filmed himself." Soon after this, the PSHE teacher left education and went to work for Staffordshire County Council. I was thrilled when I learned that, thinking that surely she would be able to add weight, having been instrumental in persuading my granddaughter to give a very personal talk to the school. I was shocked to learn that she was involved in the final decision that Ben's story was not suitable for schools.

Although Joe was spearheading the education pack, I was always busy in the background writing to people I thought could and should help with the process. Just before Christmas 2009 I wrote to the then Home Secretary, Alan Johnson, and although he didn't reply I did have some correspondence with the MP Diane Johnson, who at that time had policy responsibility for drugs education in schools. I had the same rhetoric from her that it's not up to the Government to recommend or endorse what resources are used in schools, only to set up the policy. I was then passed on to Holly Turner of the DCFS (the Department for Children, Families and Schools), who explained yet again that it isn't the department's role to deliver drugs education, only to support the delivery of it. She recognised, however, that there does need to be a means of alerting schools and local authorities to these resources so that they can decide what to use and how to use them. Holly had had a recent meeting with Andrew Brown of the Drugs Education Forum, a government agency, to see how they could best help with this task. The Drugs Education Forum had agreed to do a 'scoping' exercise to identify the scale of the job. I was upset with the response, not least because it had taken the DCSF five months for the department to tell me this, and what even is a 'scoping' exercise? At the end of the day, whose decision is it to decide what is recommended? I thought drugs education was all part of the new strategy that had to date launched anti-bullying, anti-abuse and others, and wasn't it the DCFS that had endorsed the group N-Dubz for their anti-bullying campaign?

What upset me most, however, was the fact that Ed Balls and the DCFS had publicly stated that the view of parents and young people would be listened to by government and clearly this is not the case here. I know that there will be a lot of resources in the pipeline, with more yet to be developed, and I am not naïve, there will be a lot of money in it for some, but Ben's resource was ready and has cost virtually nothing except my son's life and my peace of mind. I felt very let down by the DCFS.

Following on from the response I had from the MP Diane Johnson, I wrote to Andrew Brown at the Drugs Education Forum, and was delighted when a meeting was set up for him to come to Stafford on the 21st July 2010 and talk to Joe about the pack. He also said he would like to meet with me and I was invited to go along to the Council offices at a time when the meeting would have ended.

I went to the Council offices as instructed, had a long wait and was then told the meeting was at Starbucks! It would take another twelve months before I got to see the inside of the Council offices. It was difficult getting a word in with Andrew, but I think I managed to get all the salient points across. He said he was impressed with the education pack, although he had some reservations. Believe it or not, until that day in Stafford he hadn't seen the documentary, but now having viewed it had found it quite shocking. This is a man whose job it is to look at what's out there in resource material! He did say that children of 14-16 aren't into heroin, so would they relate Ben's story to anything they could/would experience? This is probably correct, but Ben's story is so much more than about heroin addiction, it covers other drug taking including alcohol abuse but more importantly it shows Ben's remorse at having hurt the people he loved. He didn't die of an overdose, he died through long term abuse, for want of a better way of describing it, as did Max. his friend who spoke in the Sky documentary, and Amy Winehouse too, I suspect. The body can only take so much.

Andrew agreed to the pack going out into Staffordshire in the autumn with one proviso. No school would be allowed to have the pack unless they commit the teacher delivering it to four half-days of training. There would be an assessment exercise on its success with pupils/teachers/parents, and when this assessment is complete, possibly six months after delivery, Andrew wanted Joe to present the pack to a panel in London who are experts at knowing what's effective in the drugs education field. On his return back to his office, Andrew emailed me his best wishes for the launch later in the year.

Chapter 15

In September, it became clear that the launch would not be taking place in November 2010, and I became disheartened and convinced that it was never now going to take place and that the council would shelve the pack without proceeding with its development. Joe tried to reassure me that, although there had been a number of disappointing setbacks, he was still confident that it would happen. He had spoken to key people within the Education Transformation Division and Staffordshire Young People's Service, and stressed that all were still keen to see the pack used in schools and other relevant agencies. However, they had to get it right, and if that meant it would take longer then we had to accept this in order to get good drugs education to our young people. He assured me that since we had started out on this venture many things had been achieved, including:

- *Support had been gained from the council's elected members including those that sit in the Cabinet*
- *Funding had been secured from the Youth Opportunity Fund to appoint a project manager and other services*
- *4000 of Staffordshire's young people had responded to a survey*
- *Overwhelming backing had been given by the Staffordshire Young People's Service and the Education Transformation Division*

- *20 young people had been involved in the development of the education pack which included piloting it with other young people*

Only minor changes were now needed to get it right.

There had also been a general election in 2010, with a new MP dealing with drugs issues, and I had to accept that what was in the pipeline for drugs education was dropped. We were back at square one again, with real cutbacks and a big problem with funding. I also had to accept that Ben's story would never get into the national curriculum, and that it would be up to the local education authorities as to whether or not they decided to use it given the knowledge that teachers have to be trained to deliver it.

I had one last crack at the Government. In January 2011 I wrote to James Brokenshire, the new Minister for Crime Prevention with responsibility for the new Government Drug's Strategy, as I was particularly impressed with a television news interview he gave on the subject. He wrote me a very nice letter (they all do), but again said that it was up to the local education authorities to decide what to put into their schools. Why not an overall resource available to each and every school? He told me to contact a Claire Harman from his department, which I duly did, but never received a reply.

I was getting more and more frustrated. DAT, who now go under the name of the Substance Misuse Commissioning Team, brought out a report for 2010/2011, which contained a list of achievements including:

"Developed a drugs education programme led by the UK Youth Parliament member for North Staffordshire."

How can this be listed as an achievement? It reads as if it has been successfully implemented!

In 2010, the Chairman of the Public Accounts Committee who report on the financial management of the Ministry of Justice revealed that drug use costs our society £15 billion a year and the Government spends £1.2 billion a year on a range of initiatives, as well as that of the 195,000 addicts that underwent treatment the previous year only 1 in 20 came out of treatment clean. The answer has to be in education.

I think all and sundry were relieved when I went off for a month to New Zealand in February. To be honest, I was quite exhausted, and my general health was not good. My blood pressure was consistently too high and I generally felt not at my best. I felt now I had done all I could.

When I got back home again at the beginning of March, something really nice happened for me. Nice things happen all the time around Ben's documentary, they have done since it was first broadcast by Sky. YouTube and Ben's Facebook page bring me personal messages regularly, and in March I was contacted by the playwright, David Eldridge. David was in the process of having one of his plays staged at the Almeida Theatre that month, called 'The Knot of the Heart'. It was about a young female children's television entertainer who was a heroin addict. The actress who David had written the part for, Lisa Dillon, had seen 'Ben: Diary of a Heroin Addict' on YouTube and had drawn David's attention to it. The cast had come together to watch it and David said it had influenced their performances. I was pleased because the problem was more and more being brought into the public domain. People had to address the issue more publicly, and the days of secrecy were in the descent.

Carmen, the worker who got me involved with Young Offenders, persuaded me to go to London to see it, and she would take me there. It was a great experience for me, although a little fraught at times. We got to the theatre with about a minute to spare before curtain up, as parking was a nightmare. Carmen had to throw herself on the goodness of a local resident to park on the restricted area in front of a private house. It took us five hours to get back home – Carmen's sense of direction is even worse than mine. It was worth it. The play was quite emotionally draining and when the girl, Lucy, says to her mother, "I love you Mummy," and the mother says "I love you Lucy," over and over again, I could hear Mike and Ben saying, "I love you Dad," and, "I love you Ben." If only love were enough, my family would never have had the problem.

After the performance, David had asked the cast if they would meet me and they very kindly did. Carmen and I had a great hour and a half with them in the bar, talking about the play and the problem – I think they threw us out in the end so that they could close the bar. I was disappointed that David hadn't been able to make it but, lo and behold, he came to see me two weeks later and we spent three hours talking like old friends. When he left, he asked me to take him to the cemetery so that he could pay his respects to Ben. Thank you David for all your kindness. I follow your career path and take great delight at each and every success that you have had since and that I know you will have in the future. 'The Knot of the Heart' was nominated for best play in the London Evening Standard Theatre Awards.

Chapter 16

Back to reality, and I think that by now I had accepted that the education pack was never going to happen. I felt that I had done all that I could, given the constraints, to get it into schools, and time was moving on. It was nearly five years since Ben had died and I was physically and mentally tired. I was living with Ben in my head incessantly and I know it was having an effect on my general health.

Joe called a meeting on the 16th May with Darren and I, and my daughter Sarah came along for support. The meeting was at Darren's studios in Burslem, and I guess we all knew what was coming. The Council were binning the education pack. We, of course, wanted answers, and poor Joe really was in the hot seat. These were some of the reasons that it had been rejected:

- *It would have to go before PRIDE for accreditation and it didn't meet their strict criteria*
- *No way could it be used with 14-16 year olds*
- *The DVD was the problem, it was too tough but if they got rid of the drug use/language it wouldn't be hard hitting*
- *Someone young has always been upset from seeing the DVD*
- *The teams that could offer support were no longer in place.*

- *Within prisons the support is there, within a classroom they aren't*
- *There is no money to pay outside workers, so it depends on how good the teacher is at delivering the pack. There is no guarantee that a teacher wouldn't just put the DVD on and mark papers, leaving the school children to it*
- *Young people are now saying 'no' to shock tactics*
- *Drugs education no longer compulsory, not a priority at this time*

It must have been very difficult for Joe delivering all this and I really felt for him. Although we argued around several of the reasons, it wasn't ever going to get us anywhere. Darren asked about the possibility of having the pack from the Council to try and get it out through the charitable route. Even that wasn't possible; the pack is the property of Staffordshire Council, and would be either archived or scrapped. Joe promised that the Council would write to me explaining in full why they had made the decision that they had.

Incidentally, one of the reasons given, 'that a young person has always been upset on seeing the DVD', has come up several times, and it relates to PSHE teachers in Lichfield showing the full DVD and one of their young people being traumatised by it! This is why they use the fact that there isn't the support in schools if any child is upset. I was talking to a woman recently who works in a local school and she laughed at this reasoning. She told me that they have the police going into our local schools with a DVD called 'Crash', which is about drink driving and the consequences and children have been known to have thrown up whilst watching that. I am now thinking of the young lad at the Young Offenders session where I gave a presentation, who was mightily upset when I spoke to his group. I told them about some of Ben's friends who had also died, including the one that hung himself. I am told nothing about any of the boys' backgrounds, so didn't know that this particular lad's mum had been a heroin addict and that she had hung herself. Through his tears, he thanked me for being able to talk about Ben; it was obvious that he had never been able to talk about his mum to anyone but that day all his emotions poured out. He is the one that has now turned his life around. I met him recently at an open day for the services and he gave me such a big hug. The change in his whole demeanour was heart-warming and, as upsetting as it was for me to have caused him so much distress when I went to speak to his group, I'm so glad I did.

Three days after the meeting with Joe, I couldn't believe what I was reading in our evening paper, the Sentinel. Councillor Robert Marshall, who is also the Cabinet Member for Public Health and Community Safety announced that the Council was launching a new five year plan to tackle drugs and alcohol problems across the county, which would include delivering alcohol and drugs education in schools and involving parents in some of the sessions. I was gobsmacked! The Council had taken over three years to come to the decision that for whatever reasons the education pack was not workable. The announcement of this, yet another new five years drugs strategy, had come just three days after my meeting with Joe. It seems to me that the decision not to use Ben's pack would have been made much sooner than three days earlier.

I gave the Council a further two weeks to write to me with the full explanation that Joe had promised would be forthcoming. It didn't happen, which was no great surprise to me. I think that, as far as the Council was concerned, Ben's education pack had been dealt with, they had made their decision, and common courtesy didn't come into the equation.

On the 30th May 2011, I sat down and emailed Councillor Robert Marshall, who had announced the new Drugs Strategy, the Leader of the Council Mr Philip Atkins, the Senior Advisor for Children and Young People's Personal Development and Well Being, and the ex-teacher who had persuaded Ella to do her presentation. I also emailed our local MP, Karen Bradley. I followed up this email with hard copies to all five so that I could be sure that had all received and hopefully read my letter of grievance.

My letter stated that I had met with Joe on the 16th May and been told the news that the education pack that had evolved around the documentary on my son, Ben, would not now be used by the County Council. I wrote that I was given various reasons as to its rejection and had been promised an official communication from them, for which I was still waiting. I had then learned from the Sentinel newspaper just three days later of the Council's new five year plan to tackle drugs and alcohol problems across the county which would include delivering alcohol and drugs education in schools and involving parents in some of the sessions.

I pointed out that the whole exercise that had taken place over the past three years was clearly a waste of public time and money. It had involved taking on board the views of 28 young volunteers. Was the whole project just an exercise in being seen to be listening to the young, with no real intention of putting what they want into action? They said that that young people do not want shock tactics in their drugs education, when in fact the survey that was taken in the county only two years ago and responded to by nearly 4000 children stated the opposite, that they wanted the truth presented in their drugs education.

I ended the letter by saying that I was bitterly disappointed that the Council had backtracked on this, whether it be for lack of funding, although I understood that the youth services paid for the ground work on the pack and, of course, neither Darren Teale nor I have profited in any way offering the material freely, or be it for fear of criticism from parents. I asked them to do me the courtesy, given the amount of effort I had put in both physically and emotionally, of explaining to me why at this late stage the education pack had been thrown out, and of telling me exactly what where the proposals for drugs education for 11+ pupils in Staffordshire. I asked for a reply in detail in the near future.

Councillor Roberts was the only one to reply from the Council to my email and letter, and I had a very curt response from him that read as follows:

"Received and understood. I will act on this and talk with the County Commissioner (Drug Misuse) on Wednesday afternoon – Robert Marshall."

That was on the 31st May. On the 20th June, I received a reply from my local MP Karen Bradley, who agreed that all possible measures should be taken to spread awareness in schools so that young people know how destructive getting into a vicious cycle of drug dependency may be, not just for themselves but also for their relatives. Nevertheless, as an MP she had no legal power to either influence or change the decisions that Staffordshire County Council had made, but she would forward my correspondence on to the Chief Executive of Staffordshire County Council for his comments.

I contacted Joe and he told me I was emailing the wrong people and that the person I should be contacting was the Senior School Improvement Officer of Inclusion and Well Being in Education Transformation at the Council. I wrote to her on the 16th June saying that it had been a month since I had first put in my letter of concern, and that apart from Robert Marshall no one had had the grace to reply. I wrote that I was very concerned about the way the whole issue had been dealt with, although it had come as no great surprise to me; my son had no presence when he was alive, finding it very difficult to get any help at all, and at the end of day I was little more than a heroin addict's mother. I was told there would be a meeting on the 22nd June to discuss my concerns, and that I would receive a reply soon after that date.

On the 29th June, Councillor Marshall emailed me to say that the DVD was not yet suitable for them to use but that he would like to meet me personally, along with someone from Education and/or Substance Misuse and the Commissioner for Community Safety, who turned out to be ex-Superintendent Michael Harrison, the policeman who had been so helpful in those early days. Councillor Marshall said he was certain that they have a lot to learn from me and from my experiences in this field. I was very pleased that Mick Harrison would be in on the meeting, as he was so encouraging when I took the DVD to Hanley Police Station. Unfortunately, he didn't come to the meeting, only popping his head round the door to say hello.

I accepted the invitation, but asked that Darren be included in the meeting. 28th July was the date, 4.00pm the time, County Buildings in Stafford the venue. I wish I could say that I remember every detail about the meeting, but to be honest I can't. Darren joined me outside the County Buildings and I told him I felt quite ill. He asked if I wanted to cancel but I reminded him it had taken us this long to get this far and I was going to see the inside of the council building even if it killed me! Round the council table were Councillor Robert Marshall, the County Commissioner for Substance Misuse and the Senior School Improvement Officer, Darren and I, and that's it. I remember very little about the meeting because I took violently ill very early in the meeting and it had to be adjourned. They were very kind and offered to follow me home to make sure I got there, but no thank you. Darren helped me outside and. when it became increasingly obvious that I was confused and on the point of collapse, he called an ambulance and I spent six days in Stafford Hospital.

The doctor at the hospital said it was a 'viral attack', but quite honestly I think I'd hit the proverbial brick wall. It was the end of the road and I had no more energy for the fight. I owed it to the rest of my family to ease off and concentrate on getting well. However, two weeks after getting out from hospital I had a letter from Councillor Roberts trusting that my health was improved and summarising the points raised at the meeting of the 28th, all of which would be considered at the PRIDE accreditation meeting which was due to be held on the 14th September. The Chair of the PRIDE group would be writing to me separately, setting out the deliberations of the group in relation to the DVD and the final decision.

I received the findings of the PRIDE group on the 3rd November 2011, and in all of the 13 key criteria for drugs education resources Ben's story drew a negative response.

In the meantime, whilst waiting the results of the accreditation meeting, Councillor Roberts and the County

Commissioner for Substance Misuse asked if they could come along and visit me here at home. This seemed to me to be a bit over the top. Council officials taking time out of their busy schedule to bring the meeting all the way to my house! I don't really know what their motives were in coming to my home, if they were embarrassed at the way the council had addressed the whole issue and felt I hadn't been dealt with correctly, or whether they were worried that I would continue to be vocal and in turn cause them further embarrassment. I'm just not sure. Certainly Councillor Roberts pulled out all the stops, endeavouring to both flatter and charm me. When they had both arrived, Councillor Roberts dashed back to his car to retrieve something he'd forgotten. "Oh bless," I thought, "he's brought flowers." Not so, it was a handwritten letter which he handed to me, asking me to open it and read it there and then, which I duly did. As I scanned through all three pages I had to inform him that I had received this very same letter from him but in typed format a week or so earlier, except his letter was dated the 14th August and the typed version the 11th August! That flustered him, and he had to raise the charm a notch.

I had Steffi and Sarah with me for moral support, and because I was still under par I thought they might be able to clarify for me things that might have been a bit muddled in my head. Councillor Roberts tried to win over their support for the proposal he had in mind, but, as Steffi said, "My mum is her own person and knows her own mind." The gist of it was an offer of a place on their Alcohol and Drug Strategic Partnership Board as the representative of parents and carers of people with an addiction problem. There was a lot of what I felt was patronising rhetoric about 'how best could the council engage with me to utilise my invaluable experiences and how I could contribute to the strategic decision making process.' The meeting ended with me agreeing to go to their next meeting scheduled for the 16th September as an observer, only to see whether the role would interest me. On the premise that 'it's better to be in the tent peeing out than outside peeing in', I agreed I would think about it.

I'm not at liberty to talk about the board meeting that I attended as an observer except to say that there were representatives there from all the different services such as health and the police and that they all had their own agenda to put across. That meeting was held in September 2011 and it is now May 2012 and I have heard nothing further from them whatsoever, so perhaps they think they have done enough to address the fact that they had handled the matter with insensitivity and great incompetence. I would now go happily and quietly off into the sunset, content that I had done all I could to get Ben's story into education.

Chapter 17

I certainly have to accept that Ben's story will never get on to the school curriculum and I suppose I have to be content that it is being used in many different ways educationally, but at the heart of me I'm angry that drugs education is very low priority, that it's a subject given to teachers with some space in their timetable to deliver the lesson, along with other health issues, and that by and large they know little or nothing of what they are talking about.

So why have I written all this down? Partly for my family who have suffered so much over the years through Ben's behaviour. I thought it would be good for them to see the fuller story and to know how much I have tried to get the problem out into the open. There are other families, thousands of them, suffering as we have suffered. I have met many of them over the past few years, including some very inspirational mothers, parents, siblings. I am thinking especially of Elizabeth Burton Phillips, whose twin sons fell into heroin addiction at the age of 18, resulting in one of the boys hanging himself in his mid-twenties. Elizabeth has founded the very successful charity DRUGFAM which aims specifically to help families who have been bereaved. Also, the feisty Lisa Moore, who was the aunt of Hannah Meredith, the 18 year old teenager who wrote the letter addressed 'Dear Heroin' just two weeks before she overdosed and died. Lisa told me that drug addiction has reached epidemic proportions in the area of Wales in which she lives and she has started the self-help charity 'The Hannah Meredith Foundation'. They are two brilliant women giving themselves tirelessly in order to reach out to families who would otherwise have nowhere else to turn for help and support.

I wrote the book also in response to the many messages I have received from desperate, distraught parents who genuinely feel that no-one else is suffering as they are suffering. I wanted them to know they are not alone, that their loved ones' behaviour is mirrored in my son',s and that I too have gone through the despair that they are experiencing. God knows I don't have any advice or answers; there's certainly no quick fix to the problem, but I do know that something has to be done and soon. I know that all these young people messing about with drugs now will suffer from mental health issues in the future. Education has to be about reality and must be shocking to make a lasting impact on our children.

Finally, I did it for Ben, who very obviously wanted his story to get out there. He knew he had done something that would have an impact – I didn't believe him when he was alive but I have tried to make it up to him since he died. He addressed his camera as if he knew his filming would be seen by others, and when I went through his belongings after starting writing this book it was obvious that he'd also tried to put down his experiences on paper.

Eamonn Holmes, when he interviewed me on breakfast television asked, "What now Anne, what about you?" My answer at that time was, "To get Ben's story into education so that children would learn that messing about with drugs is not an option." I feel I have gone as far as I can to do this, and I have to let it go if only to let Ben go, if that makes sense.

I love you Ben. I wish I could have made it better.

Lightning Source UK Ltd.
Milton Keynes UK
UKHW020651131119
353452UK00013B/1514/P